CW00551261

The Gloster Fancy Canary

A Guide to Keeping, Breeding and Exhibiting

The Gloster Fancy Canary

A Guide to Keeping, Breeding and Exhibiting

N. J. Barrett
and
C. Blackwell

BLANDFORD

Blandford
An imprint of Cassell
Villiers House, 41/47 Strand, London WC2N 5JE

Copyright © 1990 N. J. Barrett and C. Blackwell

Distributed in the United States by
Sterling Publishing Co, Inc.
387 Park Avenue South, New York, N.Y. 10016-8810

Distributed in Australia by
Capricorn Link (Australia) Pty Ltd.
P.O. Box 665, Lane Cove, NSW 2066

British Library Cataloguing in Publication Data
Barrett, N. J.
  The Gloster fancy canary.
  1. Pets: Gloster fancy canaries. Breeding & care
  I. Title   II. Blackwell, C.
  636.6862

ISBN 0-7137-2143-x

All rights reserved. No part of this book may be
reproduced or transmitted in any form or by any means,
electronic, or mechanical, including photocopying,
recording or any information storage and retrieval
system, without permission in writing from the
publisher.

Typeset by Litho Link Ltd, Welshpool, Powys, Wales
Printed and bound in Great Britain by Biddles Ltd.,
Guildford and King's Lynn.

Contents

Acknowledgements

The authors would like to thank: David A. Corrin, BVMS, MRCVS for his advice and assistance on matters relating to the ailments of canaries; Dennis Avon for providing photographs of some outstanding specimens, all of which originate from the Glenariff Stud, and the Gloster Canary Convention, who allowed their standards, rules and drawings to be published in this book.

Additionally, thanks are due to the many breeders and exhibitors of Gloster Canaries whose encouragement and interest in this work have been invaluable.

1 Introduction

The origins of the present-day Gloster Canary date back to
1925, when Mrs Rogerson of Cheltenham exhibited some
miniature Crested Canaries at the Crystal Palace National
Show. These birds were brought to the attention of A. W.
Smith by J. McLay, the judge officiating in the crest section
on that occasion. Both agreed that the 'Miniature Crests'
were very attractive and that the concept of breeding birds to
this standard would be very appealing to many fanciers.
Generally, the breed progressed quite slowly in the early
days, but it was popular in certain local areas and, not
surprisingly, one of these strongholds was in Gloucestershire
('Gloster'), around Cheltenham. A.W. Smith therefore thought
it would be appropriate to name the 'Miniature Crests'
Gloster Fancy Canaries and this served to give the breed its
own identity.

Exhibition Standard
In addition to naming the breed, A.W. Smith also drew up an
excellent exhibition standard for the Gloster Fancy Canary.
This standard ensured that the basic features of the breed,
which distinguished Glosters from Crests, would not be lost.
The crested form of Gloster, or the Corona, is immediately
distinguishable from all other established type standard
canaries with the exception of the Crested Canary. The main
features which distinguish the Gloster from the Crested
Canary are overall size, feather quality and lively action or
movement. If a careful check had not been kept on these
aspects, Glosters could easily have been lost as a definite type
standard breed. Despite the control on size and feather
quality, it was realized that the shape of the birds need not
suffer and that it would be possible to maintain these two
features while still producing a bird of a nice rounded, well-

7

GLOSTER CORONA CANARY
Size to be to the diminutive

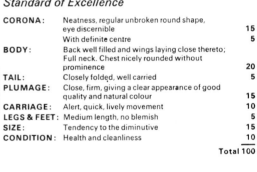

Standard of Excellence

CORONA:	Neatness, regular unbroken round shape, eye discernible	15
	With definite centre	5
BODY:	Back well filled and wings laying close thereto; Full neck. Chest nicely rounded without prominence	20
TAIL:	Closely folded, well carried	5
PLUMAGE:	Close, firm, giving a clear appearance of good quality and natural colour	15
CARRIAGE:	Alert, quick, lively movement	10
LEGS & FEET:	Medium length, no blemish	5
SIZE:	Tendency to the diminutive	15
CONDITION:	Health and cleanliness	10
		Total 100

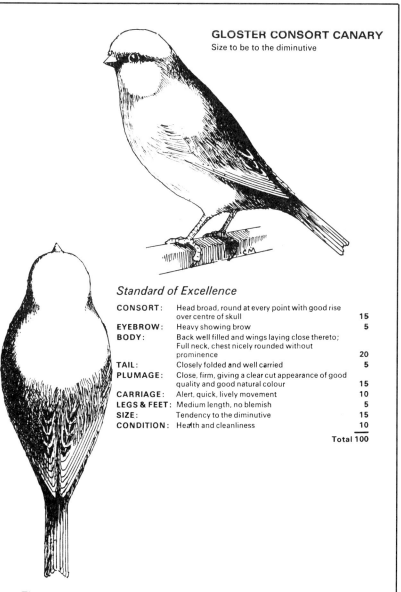

GLOSTER CONSORT CANARY
Size to be to the diminutive

Standard of Excellence

CONSORT:	Head broad, round at every point with good rise over centre of skull	**15**
EYEBROW:	Heavy showing brow	**5**
BODY:	Back well filled and wings laying close thereto; Full neck, chest nicely rounded without prominence	**20**
TAIL:	Closely folded and well carried	**5**
PLUMAGE:	Close, firm, giving a clear cut appearance of good quality and good natural colour	**15**
CARRIAGE:	Alert, quick, lively movement	**10**
LEGS & FEET:	Medium length, no blemish	**5**
SIZE:	Tendency to the diminutive	**15**
CONDITION:	Health and cleanliness	**10**
		Total 100

Fig. 1
Gloster Convention type standard drawings for the Gloster Corona and Consort, produced by Mr C. E. Minjoodt.

filled shape, or 'type'. The fact that this particular shape of bird was to be preferred, combined with the corona or crest, meant that a very different but attractive type standard canary had been 'born'.

The adoption of an excellent exhibition standard which stresses the importance of those features essential in preventing Gloster Canaries from losing their natural charm has been very important and allows the breed to realize its full potential. Additionally, the general acceptance of drawings produced by Mr C. E. Minjoodt, reproduced pp. 8-9, was a great asset in helping newcomers to the hobby visualize the ideal Gloster Fancy Canary, enabling them to set their sights on a definite goal.

Coronas and Consorts

In order to maintain Coronas it was, and still is, essential to use some non-crested birds for stock purposes. Genetically the crest is dominant in canaries and when two canaries with crests are mated together this produces undesirable results. The most serious of these is a lethal 'double factor' for crests: young with this factor usually die at a very early age, sometimes even before they hatch. In theory, 25 per cent of the young produced from a Corona × Corona mating will have a double factor for crests. Other common faults arising from this mating include skull deformities, double-centred crests and a general lack of vigour, none of which can be justified by the genuine breeder of quality stock. Once the name Corona had been given to the crested form, there could be no better name than Consort by which to refer to the non-crested birds essential for the continuation of the breed. While Consorts are very attractive birds in their own right, ideally possessing good quality of feather, neatness of size, lively movement and pleasing type, they cannot perpetuate the Gloster Fancy Canary on their own. In order to produce Coronas, one of the parents used in any mating must be a visual Corona. The only possible exception to this would be if a new recessive mutant gene for crests occurred randomly, but this is so unlikely that it can be totally discounted. Exhibition standards exist for both the Corona and the Consort, and they compete on equal terms.

The Gloster Convention

However, a charming variety of bird, an excellent exhibition standard and definitive drawings are not sufficient on their own to produce a popular breed. It is equally essential that the clubs and societies which have been formed to cater for the needs of Gloster Canary fanciers should be well organized. Specialist Gloster Canary clubs have been formed on an international, national and local level and once the beginner is ready to start exhibiting, he or she would be well advised to join at least one of these societies. The vast majority of these clubs are allied to the Gloster Convention, the governing body of the Gloster Fancy. Any changes to the show standards or the exhibition rules must be made through the Gloster Convention and all affiliated specialist Gloster clubs are allowed an equal say in any new proposals. The manner in which the Convention is constituted prevents the fancy from being manipulated by one specific society or one particularly influential fancier. Therefore it is in the best interests of all breeders keeping Gloster Canaries to ensure that the position of the Convention as the governing body remains unchallenged.

The Future

Since the early days, the Gloster Fancy Canary has steadily gained popularity; it is now the second most commonly kept type standard canary in the UK. Its development shows no signs of faltering and, in the fullness of time, it will become the number one breed, always provided that fanciers pay close attention to the written standard and use ethical breeding practices in trying to achieve this goal. Failure to pay attention to the essentials of size, feather quality and carriage would result in the production of 'monsters' with little popular appeal. The use of matings to give 'better' results in the short term, without regard to the longer-term consequences, tends to give rise to a host of congenital defects which would deter the newcomer from specializing in the breed. Without the interest at 'grass roots level', breeds tend to decline very quickly and become 'side show peculiarities' rather than 'centre stage attractions'.

2   The Gloster Canary

Before deciding to specialize in any form of type standard canary, it is essential to know, and recognize instinctively, the fundamental features of the breed. While some Gloster Canaries possess a crest, making them very different from other canaries, there are many other characteristics of the breed which are equally important, and without these no bird can be regarded as a good Gloster Canary. Failure to pay attention to these features will severely restrict your chances of breeding good-quality specimens and lead to disappointment on the show bench.

Type or Shape
The type or apparent shape of any Gloster Canary is extremely important and the requirements are the same for both the Corona and the Consort. The immediate impression should be one of neatness coupled with compactness and roundness. The head and body of the bird should appear to be one unit with no discernible neck. The Gloster Canary is not a 'head and body' bird, in which these two elements are clearly separated by a visible neck, or narrowing of outline contours, as in the case with the Border Canary for example. In the Gloster Canary it should be impossible to say where the head and body actually start and finish by visual inspection alone. In addition to being compact, the Gloster Canary must also have roundness when viewed from all angles.

The bird's body should be full and round from the beak right through to the underside of the tail. It should maintain a clean, well-defined outline right through the legs, with no apparent coarseness or roughness. The chest should be well rounded both from top to bottom and also from side to side, giving an impression of fullness with no hint of angularity.

A Flighted Three Parts Dark Buff Corona hen which was Best Gloster Canary and Best Canary at the National Exhibition of Cage Birds in 1983. The record number of this bird is 4716 and it was bred in 1982. This bird features in the pedigrees of both the Cinnamon Consort hen, record number 6368, and the Variegated Buff Corona cock, record number 5987, whose photos appear in the colour section.

Square-chested individuals do not conform to the standard. This fault is generally due to too much fat being stored by the bird. A diet too rich in fats may be responsible for this effect, but once birds have laid down excessive fat, it is very difficult to move it. Indeed the tendency to store fat may well be genetic and therefore needs to be avoided in stock birds.

While excessive chestiness must be avoided, so too should a lack of substance, which gives the birds a thin or racy appearance. Birds which lack fullness of body offer very little scope for the breeder of good-quality Glosters. The outline of the back, from the head to the tail, is the only contour which should be almost straight. It is not desirable for birds to be either hump-backed or hollow-backed.

In addition to looking at birds in profile, in the classic exhibition stance, you should also assess their appearance from the front and from above. Once again, in both cases the immediate impression should be one of compactness and roundness. There should be no narrowness around the neck, nor should there be any flatness of outline contours.

Wings and Tail

The wings and tail are extremely important in maintaining the overall impression of compactness, roundness and neatness. Any fault in the wing carriage will tend to spoil the outline of the bird. Drooping wings and crossed wings must be avoided: they are extremely difficult faults to eradicate from a stud of birds and are totally out of keeping with the basic concept of neatness. These faults also detract from the overall impression of roundness, as they break the natural contours of the bird. Birds with disproportionately long flight feathers must be avoided, as this is a clear indication that they have lost their compactness and will tend to produce youngsters which are much too long. Even where wings are of the correct length, birds can be spoilt by showing boxed, or dropped, secondaries. This means that instead of the secondary feathers being folded neatly above the longer primary flight feathers, they no longer maintain their natural position and drop down, partly obscuring the primaries. Many Gloster Canaries are spoilt by poor wings, mainly due to breeders ignoring the importance of feather quality.

The tail is just as important to the bird's appearance as the wings. Any fault in tail carriage, whether it is a drooping tail or a 'robin' tail, where it is carried at an excessively high angle, will spoil the overall type of the bird. The tail should be carried at a natural angle in line with the back and should not be too long. Beware of birds which do not have their full complement of twelve tail feathers, or those which have had their tails artificially shortened by being trimmed. The tail should be neat and compact. Fish-tailed birds, whose tail feathers are spread out sideways, are most undesirable, as are birds whose tail feathers do not lie closely together, one on top of the other, making the tail look thick. Once again poor tails are a sign of lack of attention to feather quality.

Quality of Feather

This feature is absolutely essential if the neatness which must be embodied in a good Gloster Canary is to be maintained. The only way to control the quality of feather produced in birds is to use some birds of the yellow type of feather in breeding programmes. In the quest for the ideal Gloster Canary, birds of the buff type of feather cannot by themselves achieve the ultimate goal.

The first sign of poor feather quality is excessive length and looseness of feather around the flanks. More severe problems are apparent if birds have poor wings, thick tails, coarseness of feather around the legs and roughness in the face. Generally birds which display good natural colour will also have good feather quality. To ignore the importance of feather quality is to admit that the Gloster Canary should look like the Crested Canary, and this would in turn be to show complete disregard for the original concept of the breed as it was first envisaged.

Eyes, Beak, Feet and Legs

The eyes are particularly important as it is by making eye contact that the human race develops relationships. The eyes of the Gloster Canary should be bright, round, alert and pleasing to look at. Birds which seem to squint, have a pained expression or small 'piggy' eyes are generally unattractive and probably have some disorder of the eyes. You should be aware that canaries can suffer from blindness and this complaint is probably hereditary. Birds which appear to have a white spot in the centre of the eye, or seem to lack direction in their gaze, should be avoided. Where blindness occurs in just one eye, birds will tend to point the good eye towards the observer; therefore if a bird favours one particular side, be sure to examine its other eye. The beak of a Gloster Fancy Canary should be small, neat and short, showing no signs of damage, deformity or disease. Any abnormality in the beak will destroy the proportions of the bird. Equally, feet should not show any deformities and the bird must appear to be comfortable in its stance, perching positively and showing no reluctance to display its natural action, moving from perch to perch without any need for encouragement. The legs must be neat, short and fine, with no suspicion of thigh or shank. The legs and feet should, once again, complement the overall neatness and compactness of the breed.

Carriage or Action

The Gloster Canary should appear to be robust and healthy at all times, with no tendency to lethargy. It must be alert and jaunty in action, showing no clumsiness or ungainliness. As previously mentioned, in order to be jaunty in action it is essential that birds have sound, healthy feet. While lethargic birds are to be avoided, so are those of a nervous disposition, such as 'wing shakers' and those which rarely stand still long enough to be assessed properly.

Temperament

The temperament of birds used to found an exhibition stud is extremely important. Birds of a nervous disposition and flighty nature tend to produce youngsters with the same undesirable characteristics. Good temperament must be established in any stud which is going to be successful on the show bench. This steadiness needs to be bred into birds by avoiding the use of any birds which refuse to perform properly in a show cage. Nervous tendencies to beware of include clinging to the wires of the cage front, continually shaking the wings as if about to take flight, or perpetually circumnavigating the show cage as if the perches were too hot to touch.

While good temperament can be bred into birds, it can be destroyed by careless handling. Clumsiness or suddenness of movement in the birdroom will tend to unsettle birds. If they are handled roughly during their initial show training, young birds will soon become wary of the show cage and consequently fail to perform naturally when being judged. A judge seldom has time to allow nervous birds more than a few minutes to gain their composure and certainly cannot assess anything which does not stand still.

Tendency to the Diminutive

In addition to attempting to combine all the previously mentioned desirable features, it is essential that the 'finished product' is a small bird. When breeding birds to the type or shape desired in Gloster Canaries, that is to say a full round bird with substance, there is always a tendency for them to become larger overall. This tendency must be monitored carefully, for whatever else a Gloster Canary may be, it certainly should not be a big bird. The standard Gloster show cage provides a 'measuring stick' by which to determine accurately the length and size of any bird within that cage. The 'measuring stick' is achieved by the perches in the cage, which are positioned exactly 3 in (7.5 cm) apart from centre to centre. When a bird stands naturally on one perch, and faces towards the end of the show cage nearest to it, i.e. directly away from the other perch, ideally its tail should not overhang the perch on which it is not standing. The amount by which the tail overhangs the perch indicates clearly how oversized any individual bird may be. Unfortunately many beginners tend to buy big birds, perhaps in the belief that they are getting more for their money. In order to keep birds to the correct size it is generally necessary that all hens used for stock purposes tend to the diminutive. Stronger, slightly larger cock birds of a more masculine appearance can be used successfully in breeding programmes provided they are mated to small, neat hens.

Corona and Consort
All the points discussed in this chapter apply equally to both the Gloster Corona and the Gloster Consort. The only difference between these two types of birds is the arrangement of the feathers on the head. Your aim should therefore be to produce a stud of Gloster Canaries where all birds attain the same standard of excellence with regard to type, size, feather quality and carriage, regardless of whether they are Coronas or Consorts. While Gloster Canaries must have good head qualities in order to compete on the show bench, this feature must be combined with all the other required essentials if a specimen is going to be held up as being a good example of an exhibition Gloster Canary.

3 The Corona

The Gloster Corona differs from the Gloster Consort only in that the Corona has a crest and the Consort does not. In all other respects the two birds should be identical: they should possess the same type, the same quality of feather, the same size and the same action. It is quite possible, however, to breed canaries with many different shapes and types of crest, but only one of these matches the standard set within the Gloster Fancy.

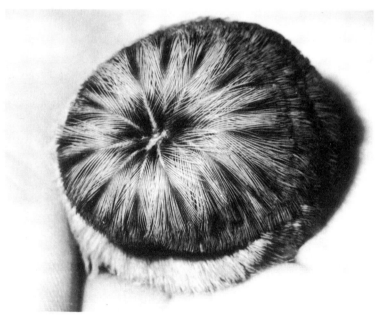

A close-up of the head qualities of an outstanding Gloster Corona, showing the evenness and neatness of the crest.

The Ideal Corona

The crest displayed by the ideal Gloster Corona should be circular in shape, showing neatness and regularity throughout. It must have a definite centre and the plumage should radiate uniformly, directly away from the crest centre, in all directions, showing no breaks or splits in any part of the crest. The feathers in the crest are also required to have some droop, so that the crest follows the contours of the head and does not stick out sideways like a frying pan. The back of the crest must blend in uniformly with the head and neck, maintaining the neatness essential to the breed. The crest also requires fullness at the sides to enable the back of the crest to blend in with head and neck. When the bird is viewed from the side, at eye level, the eye should be visible to the observer. The plumage present in the crest should be adequate to provide the desired effect without being unmanageable and must fall neatly and naturally into place, showing no tendency to lift up from the head. Breeders must strive to maintain neatness and form in the crest at all times and refuse to use birds with undesirable crest faults, no matter what other desirable features may be present in these birds.

Common Faults

The faults that can be produced in the Corona are countless. Some of the more common faults are as follows.

The displaced centre, where the middle of the crest is not central to the head: this displacement can be forwards, backwards or sideways, and is generally associated with birds of poor pedigree. Birds of this type are useless for producing exhibition Gloster Coronas.

The double centre crest, where there is more than one definite centre: again this is associated with birds of poor pedigree, and birds showing this fault must not be used in any stud of exhibition Glosters.

The parted crest, where instead of having a definite centre the crest has a parting, either from back to front or from side to side: again this makes a bird a 'non-starter' in the production of exhibition-quality Glosters and it must be discarded.

The short crest, where the crest, particularly at the front, is too short, so that it looks more like a crew-cut than a cap:

these birds are useless in establishing a stud of exhibition Gloster Canaries and indicate a lack of pedigree in their parents.

The 'punk crest', where the feathers grow in all directions, including straight up in the air: such birds are often produced when birds from different studs are mated together. If such a pairing produces one bird with a good crest and one with a 'punk crest', it is quite in order to retain the bird with the good crest for future breeding programmes. Such birds should produce a larger proportion of good crests as the stud becomes established. Birds which display a 'punk crest' are of no use at all in producing exhibition Glosters.

The frosted crest, in dark crested birds, where all the feathers in the crest have frosted edges: this is a clear indication that the general feathering of the bird has become much too coarse. When the feather has reached this stage it is usually too late to try and improve feather quality by using yellow-feathered birds.

The mop top, where there is excessive length in the crest, often coupled with a lack of definite centre, and general untidiness: while some fanciers may seek excessive crests, it should be remembered that long head-feathers cannot be coupled with short feathers in the tail, and therefore birds will tend to be too big and generally lack neatness. Should fanciers prefer this type of bird they would perhaps be better looking to the Crested Canary Fancy rather than to the Gloster Canary Fancy.

The frying-pan crest, where the feathers stick out sideways and do not follow the contours of the head, making the crest look flat: birds with this fault are usually bred by mating Coronas to Consorts which have excessive feather on the head, similar to the Crest Bred birds generally associated with the Crested Canary Fancy.

The horned crest, where a number of feathers at the back of the crest, usually at both sides, stick out and spoil the overall neatness: this fault is often produced by pairing Coronas to Consorts which have flat-sided heads or Consorts which have horns themselves. It may also be associated with pairings involving birds of the yellow-feather type. The fault is difficult to eradicate and where the use of yellow-feathered birds is responsible, the answer must lie in obtaining or breeding yellows of a better type, especially with regard to their head qualities.

The hairy crest, where the plumage of the entire crest seems to lack body and is generally of a 'flyaway' nature: this is due to the bird possessing feather which is too fine, and breeders should look to increase the body of the feather. This can usually be achieved by pairing these birds to buff-feathered birds, even if this entails mating buff to buff. However, do not be tempted to use birds of the coarse buff-feather type to rectify the fault instantly; be patient and increase the body of the feather gradually.

The split crest, where there appears to be a gap in one section of the crest, as if some feathers were missing: should this occur at the front of the crest it is best to avoid using any birds with this fault for stock purposes. If the split occurs at the side of the crest, and the bird is good in other respects, it could be used occasionally for stock purposes, if there is no better alternative available.

The bald-necked Corona, where there is a significant bald patch at the base of the skull that spoils the lie of the feathers, creating a gap in the plumage at the back of the neck which can be seen by visual inspection alone. Provided these birds are good in other respects, and no better alternative is available, they can be used sparingly, and the best chance of improvement probably lies in using Consorts of a better type, especially with regard to compactness of head and body.

The whorled crest, where the plumage seems to rotate slightly around the centre of the crest, so that it is not exactly symmetrical: this is not a serious fault in breeding stock, provided birds with this style of crest are used only very sparingly in breeding programmes.

The Quest for Perfection

It might seem that with so many common faults the task of breeding good Coronas is virtually impossible. However, the breeding of any form of livestock to exhibition standards is always difficult, otherwise it would be a pointless exercise. Provided breeders search continually for neat-crested birds with good, definite crest centres, and pay attention to feather quality at all times, the percentage of faulted crests produced should be reduced with each successive breeding season. In the fullness of time, when a well-founded stud has been established – and this cannot be achieved overnight – the numbers of birds being bred with serious crest faults should be a very small proportion of the total number of birds produced. It is, however, always essential to be very careful when selecting birds for stock purposes.

4 The Consort

As previously mentioned, the Gloster Corona Canary cannot be perpetuated without the use of non-crested birds in breeding programmes. These birds are called Gloster Consorts and they owe their existence to the Corona. Despite the fact that, ideally, Consorts are very attractive, charming little birds of good type and quality, they have been developed expressly for the purpose of being suitable breeding partners for Coronas. Therefore, no matter what other features the bird possesses, a good exhibition Consort should have the visual attributes which would be capable of producing good-quality Gloster Corona Canaries. The concept of there being one style of Consort for breeding Coronas and another style for exhibition and breeding Consorts is quite misguided.

Once again, as the only difference between the Consort and the Corona lies in the feathering on the head, we are primarily concerned with head characteristics in this chapter.

The Ideal Consort
The head of the Consort should be round when viewed from the side, the front and directly from above. From the side there should be a good rise from the beak, over the centre of the skull, with the natural line of curvature continuing until it blends smoothly into the neck and back. The throat should be full so that there is no sharpness under the beak and all outlines should flow naturally into the body of the bird, emphasizing the compactness of the breed. From the front, the head should appear rounded, from eye to eye, with no flatness across the top of the head. There must be width between the eyes, with no hint of narrowness in the head. The cheeks should be full, without any hollowness, blending neatly into the shoulders. From above, the head should be as broad as it is long, so that is it circular in outline. While the

An example of a quality Variegated Buff Consort hen of the style required in a good stud of Gloster Canaries.

exhibition standard asks for Consorts to show brow, this must not be so pronounced that it obscures the eyes. The head of the Gloster Consort must be in proportion to the body: birds which have disproportionately large heads do not comply with the exhibition standard.

Common Faults

There are many head faults which can totally spoil the potential of Consorts, both as show birds and stock birds. It is not possible to itemize every single fault that can occur, but some of the more common serious faults are as follows.

Narrowness in any part of the head is most undesirable in any Gloster Consort. This can usually be seen most clearly when birds are viewed from the front or from directly above. When viewing from the front, narrowness between the eyes and narrowness in the face are the two most obvious faults. From directly above, narrowness at the back of the skull, the front of the skull or the whole of the skull becomes apparent. Oval heads indicate narrowness of the skull generally, while egg-shaped heads indicate narrowness of the front skull or back skull. Breeding from Consorts whose heads are not circular in outline severely restricts the possibility of producing Coronas with circular crests.

Flatness in the head, when the bird is viewed in profile or directly from the front, must also be avoided. The contour of the head must rise from the beak and continue in a uniform curve to the back of the head. From the front, the head should be rounded and not flat across the top. A lack of roundness in the Consort's head will be detrimental to the shape and style of the crests displayed by Coronas bred from it. Flatness or hollowness in the face is also undesirable and is often associated with a lack of back skull. This spoils the overall effect of roundness and will also limit the potential of any Coronas which may be bred from birds of this style.

Lines or grooves in the head plumage, which generally run from the eyes to the back of the head, are a feature to be avoided in all Consorts. Not only do these lines spoil the appearance of Consorts, they are also a clear indication that the plumage around the head does not grow naturally in the desired direction. If this feature was passed on to young Coronas bred from a Consort with this fault, it would be detrimental to the shape and neatness of their crest. Horns caused by small feathers, also growing in the wrong direction, at the back of the head, again spoil the appearance of the Consorts themselves and will also tend to be passed on to Coronas produced from these birds. It may be tempting to remove these errant feathers for exhibition purposes, but remember, you cannot alter the breeding characteristics of a bird with scissors or tweezers.

'Top lifters' are birds which persistently raise the feathers on top of the head, as if slightly startled. Obviously such birds will have disastrous effects if used to produce Coronas, as they will also tend to indulge in this undesirable behaviour.

Meanness of expression, apart from being caused by narrowness of skull, can be due to sharpness under the beak. This sharpness is generally caused by birds lacking fullness in the throat and will obviously spoil the overall appearance of the bird. Again this fault will tend to be passed on to any offspring produced from such a bird, perhaps not in the first generation, but certainly in future generations, and should therefore be avoided.

Excessive feather on the head is another undesirable feature in the Gloster Consort Canary, primarily because this feature totally alters the original concept of the breed. While some judges and exhibitors may tend to favour Consorts of this style, they are doing the Gloster Fancy a disservice. The Consort exists to produce good-quality Coronas, and Consorts with excessive head feather cannot be used successfully to achieve this goal. It is rather like trying to wear a hat on top of a beehive hairstyle – totally ridiculous!

The Quest for Perfection
Ideally the feathering on the head of a Consort should tend to grow towards the sides of the head, but not to such an extent that the eyes become obscured. This tendency to sideways growth of the feather lends itself more readily to producing crests of the desired neatness and form than does feathering which aligns itself lengthways along the head from front to back. However, it is important not to look for just one specific feature when founding a stud. The beginner must view birds offered for sale as a complete unit, and not be tempted to risk using a bird which excels in some respects but is seriously faulted in others. Many different styles of birds are offered for sale as Gloster Consorts and breeders will generally have more choice in the style of Consorts they can acquire than they have with Coronas. Therefore decisions as to the specific style of Consorts purchased tend to rest with the buyer. It is very important to have fixed firmly in your mind what style of Consort you require in order to have the best chance of producing both good-quality Coronas and good-quality Consorts. When in doubt, seek guidance from a more experienced neutral party, if at all possible.

5 Feather Quality

The most common reason for failing to establish a good stud of Gloster Canaries is inability to maintain feather quality. In order to establish good feather quality in any stud of exhibition canaries it is essential to understand the rudiments of the two basic feather types. The Gloster Canary is no exception to this rule, and the fact that the vast majority of Gloster Canaries are of the buff-feather type does not mean that the use of birds with the yellow type of feather is optional.

Yellow Feather
A canary which is yellow in colour is not necessarily a bird of the yellow-feather type. The type of feather usually described in canary circles as yellow tends to be a relatively hard feather which is quite narrow and has fine texture. Although narrow, yellow feather is not bound to be longer than any other type of feather. It possesses bright, natural colour which should extend right to the edges of the feather. The feather quality of good yellows must be of a silky appearance, with the plumage appearing to be one complete unit, rather than a collection of different individual feathers. Examples of yellow-feathered birds can be bred in all canaries, regardless of their colour and markings, always provided one of the parent birds is actually of the yellow-feather type. Because of the narrowness and fineness, yellow-feathered birds can appear to lack substance when compared to birds of the buff-feather type. While it may be that yellows have limited use as exhibition birds, they are essential for the control of feather quality in all studs. When mated to good-quality buff-feathered birds, yellows do not necessarily have any detrimental effect on the substance of buff-feathered birds bred from them. The breeder must, however, be aware that not all

A Self Green Yellow Gloster Consort hen, essential in the production of a top-quality stud of Gloster Canaries. The record number of this bird is 6485 and it was bred in 1988. The maternal grandfather of this bird was the father of the Variegated Buff Corona hen, record number 5907, whose pedigree sheet appears on p.180.

yellows have good feather quality. Often a yellow-feathered bird is used as a last ditch attempt to salvage something from the remnants of a stud of rough buff-feathered birds. When this is done, and yellows are produced, these birds will have many of the undesirable features associated with their buff-feathered parent. If used for breeding purposes, they will in turn pass these undesirable features on to their offspring, which is why birds with feather lumps are sometimes bred directly from yellows. Yellows are not a cure for feather lumps; they are a means by which it is possible to establish a stud which is not going to be ruined by coarseness of feather or by feather lumps. Any yellows which have thick tails, where the feathers do not lie closely together, or have plumage which shows signs of frosting will be useless for maintaining feather quality. Even if suitable yellow-feathered birds are used initially, there is no guarantee that the problem of feather lumps will be avoided. Great care must be taken in the selection of all stock, both yellows and buffs, in order to establish a sound stud of birds.

Buff Feather
The type of feather usually described in canary circles as buff tends to be a relatively soft feather which is quite broad and lacks the fineness of texture generally associated with yellow feather. Because of the soft nature of buff feather, it is more delicate and more easily damaged than yellow feathering. Colour in this type of feather is not as intense as that displayed by yellows, particularly with regard to the yellow pigment, which is present in all colours of Gloster Canary with the exception of white ground birds. The yellow pigment in buff-feathered birds does not extend right to the edges of the feather and therefore feathers on buffs have a slightly frosted appearance. The feather quality of good buffs should, however, also be of a silky appearance, and it is when this quality is lost that problems start to occur.

Examples of buff-feathered birds can be bred in all canaries, regardless of their colour and markings, and it is theoretically possible to breed buffs from a pair of yellow-feathered birds. This is because the vast majority of yellows carry the gene responsible for producing buff feather hidden in their genetic make-up. However, a pair consisting of two buffs will produce only buff birds and can never produce a yellow-feathered bird. Because of the broader nature of the feather, buff birds appear to have more type and substance than yellows. This makes them firm favourites on the show bench and accounts for the large proportion of buff-feathered birds within the Gloster Canary Fancy. When two buffs which have both been produced from yellow × buff pairings are mated together, this is termed double buffing: this practice is quite acceptable in the production of good-quality Glosters. If two buffs which have both been produced from buff × buff pairings are mated together, this is more than double buffing and should be undertaken only with great caution. The continual use of buff × buff pairings, whether these birds are Greens, Variegateds, Cinnamons, Whites or Grizzles, without the introduction of yellow-feathered birds is bound to be detrimental to feather quality and will ultimately destroy any stud of Gloster Canaries. The two main problems associated with birds produced by continually pairing buff to buff are excessive softness of feather and excessive coarseness of feather. When the feathering becomes too soft, the problem will be manifested in the form of feather lumps. When it becomes too coarse, there will be a general lack of neatness, with tails and wings being particularly badly affected. Usually these two problems accompany each other and both are impossible to rectify, unless you are prepared to sell up and start again.

Other Modifying Factors
In addition to plumage being yellow or buff, there are other factors which can affect the texture and quality of feathering. Variegated feathers, where all the colour pigments, except the yellow pigment, have been removed, will tend to be softer in texture than feathers which are not variegated. Therefore, when breeding Light Variegated birds and Grizzles, the feathering will tend to become excessively soft. The White mutation can produce a slight general softening of feather texture, but this should not be as noticeable as it is in Light Variegateds and Grizzles. The Cinnamon mutation also tends to soften feather, but additionally produces a feather which is generally finer than normal. Once again this feather needs to be carefully monitored to prevent the desired quality of feather being lost. Pairing Cinnamons to yellows, for example, will usually result in producing feather which is too fine to be of use to the breeder of exhibition Glosters. However, do not think that Cinnamons can be used as a substitute for yellows. Although Cinnamons may have the required fineness of feather, they do not have the necessary feather hardness.

Advised Procedure
The first aim when founding a stud of Glosters with good feather quality should be to establish a nucleus of buff Greens

and yellow Greens, i.e. birds which are at least Three Parts Dark or darker. The buff Greens should possess as many of the features we generally associate with good-quality Glosters as possible. These may take some finding, but as there always seems to be a surplus of buff Greens, the buyer should have the opportunity to select from a number of birds and a number of different sources. The features which must be present in the yellow Greens are good colour and good feather quality, as without these, yellows are useless as stock birds. Naturally if yellow Greens of good colour and good feather quality, which also have compactness and roundness of type, are available, these would be most desirable. To this base of Green buffs and yellows, a few individuals to provide variety, such as a Variegated buff, a Cinnamon, a Blue or even a Grizzle, can be added. Generally the breeder should try to work on the principle that buff Greens can be paired to anything, including buff Greens, but that others should not be paired to anything except a buff Green in the early stages of building up a stud.

When the buff Greens are mated to the yellow Greens this will provide yellows and buffs. The yellows will be required to maintain the stock of yellows in the birdroom which is essential to produce more buffs bred from yellows and also yellows themselves. If the original yellows were slightly lacking in compactness and roundness, the birds produced from them should be an improvement, provided suitable buff Greens were selected initially. The buffs bred from yellows should be used to improve and maintain the feather quality of the stud generally. The compactness and neatness of buff-feathered birds bred from yellow × buff matings is often quite a pleasant surprise. What breeders forget is that the lack of shape in yellows is due mainly to their feather texture, and when this texture is altered, the apparent shape of the birds produced also changes. Provided buff Greens bred out of a yellow show the features associated with good-quality Glosters, they can usefully be paired to any buff-feathered bird of reasonable quality, regardless of colour or markings. All the young produced from such a mating will be buffs. If they maintain good feather quality and colour, they can be mated to a suitable buff for one more generation, before being brought back to pair to a buff bred from a yellow, or if they are Heavily Variegated Greens or darker, directly to a yellow Green.

Dark or Light

Although most fanciers would prefer to have a birdroom full of good-quality Variegateds rather than good-quality Darks, the realistic choice is often between a birdroom full of poor-quality Variegateds or good-quality Darks. Feather quality is extremely difficult to control in Clear and Light Variegated birds. When these birds are produced in the formative years of building up a stud, it is generally advisable to pair them to buff-feathered birds which are at least Heavily Variegated, if not darker. Ideally the Dark buff used should have been bred out of a yellow to offer the best possible chance of controlling feather quality. Pairing Light Variegated to Light Variegated is very risky, especially for fanciers who do not have a great deal of experience in assessing the finer points of feather quality. It is a policy which can easily produce birds with feather problems, and this in turn can lead only to a dead end. A wiser policy is to be cautious and preserve the quality of your Clear and Light Variegated birds by mating them to darker birds. After mating Light Variegated birds to Dark birds, it may be that all the youngsters produced are Dark, but most will carry the capacity to produce Light Variegated birds in future generations. In order to achieve this it may be necessary to do some searching through breeding records to find a suitable bird to use as a mate. A bird which is the offspring of a different Light Variegated bird will usually have the best chance of revealing the variegation.

Patience

Using yellow-feathered birds to found a stud of Glosters is by no means easy. Careful selection of stock birds and years of patience are required to combine all the desirable features of good-quality Glosters throughout any stud. There are, however, no short cuts on the road to achieving the ultimate goal; risking the use of unsuitable birds is to court disaster. While the first generation youngsters produced from a bird with a feather lump, for example, may appear to have escaped scot-free, they have this undesirable feature concealed in their genetic make-up. This will in turn be passed on to their offspring, and so on, until quite suddenly the feature reappears. The longer it remains hidden the worse will be the consequences, with pair after pair producing birds with feather lumps. When previous breeding records are examined it will be found that nearly every bird in the stud is related to the bird with the original problem. In practical terms this means there will be no certain way of determining which birds carry the fault and which do not, and therefore no sure way of removing these birds from the stud, apart from disposing of all your stock.

Exceptions to Generalizations
There will always be birds that defy generalizations, such as Light Variegateds with relatively hard feather texture or Cinnamons with coarse feathering. However, there can be no exceptions to the fact that each individual bird possesses just one type of feather. It is impossible to produce a strain of birds with soft long feathers in the head and hard short feathers in the wings and tail. Breeders must accept that the best that can be achieved is one general overall feather type which is sufficiently soft to produce the desired head qualities, but not so soft that it results in feather abnormalities in the wings and tail. Neatness of feather is not just an asset to a Gloster Canary, it is essential, and it can be achieved only by careful attention to the feather quality of all birds being assessed as potential breeding stock.

6 Acquiring Stock

Having been captivated by the charm of the Gloster Fancy Canary, you may want to acquire some birds as quickly as possible. In fairness to the birds, and to your enthusiasm, you should not purchase any bird until you have made proper provision to house them correctly. Even after you have bought a suitable birdroom, it is still wise to be cautious with regard to acquiring your initial stock. For those with no experience of breeding and managing canaries, it is advisable to gain the rudiments of a practical knowledge before spending hard-earned cash on stock capable of producing exhibition-quality birds. While successful exhibitors may have full order books for their surplus stock, and therefore charge relatively high prices, many other breeders dispose of stock far more cheaply. Such birds will probably be ideally suited to the beginner, who has many lessons to learn about the practical management of canaries before being able to lay the foundations of an exhibition-winning stud.

Specialist Societies
Once the basics have been learned, the breeder can start to upgrade the quality of his or her stock. At this point it is generally worthwhile joining at least one specialist Gloster Canary society, ideally one which publishes a full list of patronage show results and a current list of members annually. Joining a specialist club too early can be detrimental to a member's exhibition status. Once a fancier has joined a specialist Gloster club he or she will automatically become a champion exhibitor five years later. If you join a club as soon as you become interested in Glosters, it is possible that you will not be ready to start exhibiting for another three years, and this would allow you only two years in the novice ranks, before you had to compete as a champion. The prospective

fancier has a great deal to learn before stepping up to champion status.

By looking at show results, visiting shows and talking to fellow Gloster fanciers, it should be possible for you to build up a mental picture of the type of birds which are required for success on the show bench. Once you are able to recognize the style of bird required, the next step is to look for exhibitors who bench this type of bird. When fanciers exhibit birds which vary markedly in size and style, this indicates that although they may possess a few good individuals, they have not, as yet, established a true breeding strain. When the newcomer has drawn up a short list of breeders who he or she thinks will offer for sale the type of birds required, he or she should contact the breeders in order to find out if surplus stock is available, and at what price it will be sold.

Viewing Stock
When you have found a breeder who can offer surplus birds for sale, you should arrange to travel to the fancier in order to view the birds on offer. Ideally you will be given a choice of a number of pairs which are surplus to requirements. However, do not think that it is possible to buy birds which have not been offered for sale: attempting to badger fanciers into selling birds they wish to keep will only make you unpopular and reduce your chances of being offered surplus stock in future years. By all means look at the stud as a whole – this

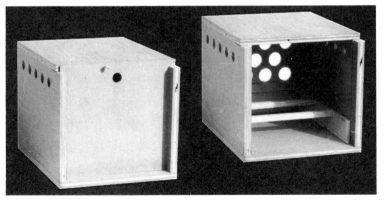

A box suitable for the transportation of canaries when birds have to be shipped over long distances to meet demands from buyers.

will give you a good idea of the overall quality of the birds maintained – but do not think that you can buy your way into the fancy. Ask questions about specific birds which you particularly like, and also ask to see close relatives of the birds which are being offered for sale. If you do not like the birds which are being offered for sale then you should be under no obligation to make a purchase. But remember that the birds which are offered for sale are unlikely to be as good as the birds being retained by seller. It would be foolish for any fancier to sell his or her best birds. What the purchaser is paying for is birds *related* to top-quality specimens, which will therefore have the potential, when correctly managed, to produce top-quality birds themselves.

Sexing
At times canaries can be difficult to sex. Generally cocks sing and hens do not, but it is probably more accurate to say that hens lay eggs and cocks do not. Some hens can string together enough notes of song to confuse even the most experienced fancier, while some cock birds are very reluctant to sing and may not actually be seen singing until early spring. In the case of over year or flighted birds, the fancier selling the birds should guarantee that they have been correctly sexed. However, with young or unflighted birds, a 100 per cent guarantee cannot always be given. It is very disappointing to buy 'pairs' of birds, only to find they are two cocks or two hens, but the acquisition of at least one flighted cock and one flighted hen should ensure that some matings can be made. If you find that birds bought as a pair are in fact of the same sex, it is worthwhile contacting the fancier from whom they were bought; in the vast majority of cases he or she will try to remedy the situation if at all possible. Buying birds wearing a precisely numbered identification ring is a good policy as this means both the buyer and the seller will be sure of the origins of any problem birds.

After-care
From whatever source you buy birds, they should be housed separately from all other birds for at least two weeks. During this period they should be treated with mite powder and observed closely to ensure they are showing no signs of

illness or disease which could be passed on to other stock. Birds you already own, which have reared youngsters successfully during the 'apprenticeship period', should be retained for the following breeding season. The birds purchased may breed perfectly well in another establishment, but might not be so productive when kept and maintained in a different system. Proven breeders are often very useful as foster parents if problems arise with the rearing duties of the better-quality newly introduced birds. Using foster parents in the early stages of founding a strain should not cause too many problems later, as the birds reared in your own birdroom will tend to adapt more easily to your system than will birds introduced from other sources. Generally speaking, pedigree livestock is more difficult to breed from than non-pedigree stock.

Instant Success
Breeding good-quality birds does not just entail buying birds from a reputable source and producing youngsters from them. Occasionally newly acquired stock will produce outstanding youngsters immediately, but more often the task of breeding quality birds requires a little more work on the part of the breeder. It is foolish to part with youngsters bred from good birds just because they are not class winners. These birds must be given the opportunity to prove themselves and they can do this only if they are allowed to breed. Very often birds take after their grandparents rather than their parents, and it is for this reason that fanciers seek out breeders with birds of a consistent quality rather than those with one or two 'stormers' and a shed full of 'also rans'.

7 Housing

Before actually acquiring any birds it is essential to have at your disposal suitable quarters in which to house them. This may seem to be a blatantly obvious statement, but it is surprising just how many people buy birds on impulse without having made proper provision for their accommodation. Birdrooms, cages and aviaries which are hurriedly constructed, without careful forethought and planning, seldom cater adequately for the birds they are meant to house.

The Birdroom
For anyone hoping to establish a stud of quality Glosters the

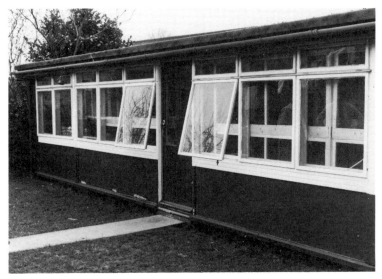

An exterior view of the birdroom used by Nick and Annalain Barrett to house the 'Glenariff' stud of Gloster Canaries.

first consideration must be the provision of a birdroom. The
design and position of the birdroom must be given careful
consideration in order to realize the full value of the
investment made. The majority of birdrooms are of timber
construction, although brick-built birdrooms can be just as
effective. The quality of the materials and the standards of
workmanship employed in constructing a birdroom are very
important, and short-term economies may well prove to be
long-term liabilities. Damp, draughty birdrooms which
permit easy access for vermin are totally unsuitable for
canaries. Any time and money saved initially by 'cutting
corners' can prove very costly in the long term and may be
responsible for unacceptably high mortality rates among the
stock maintained, poor breeding results both with regard to
quantity and quality, excessive time wasted in trying to keep
the structure adequately maintained and a general disenchant-
ment with the hobby on the part of the birdkeeper. Naturally
the ease with which you are able to attend to the day-to-day
general management of your stock greatly affects the
pleasure you derive from keeping birds.

Birdrooms must be sited on firm level ground which is
free from standing water and they should have properly
constructed foundations. Timber birdrooms need to be
treated with wood preservative on a regular basis in order to
prevent any rot developing. The undersides of wooden floors
are particularly susceptible to rot and must be thoroughly
treated before being laid. It is also essential to leave some
clearance between the ground and the floor, so that air can
circulate freely under the birdroom to prevent excessive
dampness. Naturally the floor of the birdroom must be
supported at regular intervals to prevent sagging, but by
leaving a clearance of about 9 in (22.5 cm), it is possible
without too much difficulty to take effective measures for the
removal of any unwanted residents who may establish a
home under the birdroom.

The roof of a birdroom is a potential source of trouble.
Should the roof start to leak, major reconstruction work is
often needed to remedy the fault. Initially it may seem like a
good idea to incorporate windows in the roof of the birdroom, thus allowing additional free wall space inside. In
theory the idea may seem excellent, but in practice it is often

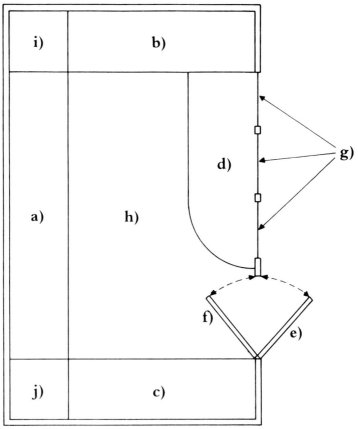

Fig. 2
Possible layout options for a birdroom: a) space for breeding cages; b) and c) space for inside flight, breeding cages, show preparation cages or storage; d) space for seating or storage; e) exterior door; f) interior wire safety door; g) windows; h) floor space; i) and j) space necessarily wasted when cages are positioned on adjacent walls.

the cause of unwanted and time-consuming problems. Skylights are notorious for leaking and should this occur the only effective remedy might be to replace the roof completely. However, once the decision to include windows in the roof has been taken, the new roof will also require windows, unless additional windows can be incorporated elsewhere in the existing structure. Windows in roofs also provide excellent viewing galleries for cats, which does nothing to improve the confidence of your birds. The steadiness and contentment of the birds may also be disturbed by the shadows cast by wild birds passing overhead. Roofs must be properly protected by good-quality roofing felt and may also be further protected with tar and white stone chippings. The white stone chippings will help to reflect heat in the summer and prevent the roof acting as a large heater radiator.

Generally it is advisable to site birdrooms so that they face east; this gives the birds the benefit of good natural light in the early morning and protects them from the heat of the midday sun in summer. Birdrooms usually benefit by being shaded from the full effects of the sun. In addition, the windows of the birdrooms must be able to be opened. This helps to control temperature and can also prevent birds from being brought into breeding condition too quickly during the winter months. A few sunny days in late winter can soon raise the birdroom temperature and fool both the birds and the birdkeeper into thinking the breeding season is imminent. Opening the windows daily, throughout the year, will help to modify the temperature within the birdroom and allow birds to build up more gradually and naturally to full breeding condition. All windows must be protected by removable wire netted frames fixed to the interior wall of the birdroom, not only to prevent birds being accidentally lost through open windows, but also to keep out vermin. Equally, if the birdroom door is going to be left open to provide additional ventilation, then a wire door should be used as a replacement.

Usually all the windows will be on one wall of the bird-room, and a more effective use of the interior space available is often achieved by having the door in the same wall as the windows. This leaves three complete interior walls free for cages and other fixtures and fittings.

Most birdroom interiors will need to be lined throughout, with wall boards or similar materials, before being ready for the installation of any cages. Good insulation will help to prevent sudden temperature changes within the birdroom and also eliminate unwanted draughts, and some form of insulation should be placed on the inside of the roof and all walls, prior to fixing the lining. A stuffy atmosphere is not, however, suitable for keeping canaries fit and healthy and therefore, having insulated and lined the birdroom, it is essential to provide adequate ventilation. This can be achieved in part by opening the windows and door of the birdroom, but will often need to be complemented by the provision of permanent ventilators or extractor fans in the fabric of the birdroom.

When the floor is laid it may be advisable to cover the entire interior surface with ½ in (12 mm) wire netting and then cover this with material such as chipboard. The wire net will provide a deterrent to small vermin and the 'false floor' will prevent the floor proper from being continually dampened by your birds bathing. Before the 'false floor' is fitted the interior surface of the real floor will need to be treated with an effective wood preservative, as will the 'false floor', which will require additional retreating on a regular basis. When the 'false floor' is being treated in an established birdroom, adequate ventilation is essential as the fumes from these chemicals can be harmful to birds. Creosote is quite suitable as a preservative, given that adequate precautions have been taken, and offers effective protection at a sensible price.

Generally, the larger the birdroom the more difficult it is to maintain and manage. For the beginner it would be wise to start with a birdroom of reasonable proportions, about 10 ft (3 m) × 6 ft (1.8 m), and accept that a larger structure may be required in the future. Some initial practical experience is essential if you are to avoid the possible pitfalls of a large birdroom. When assessing the number of birds which can be housed in a birdroom, remember that not only breeding stock must be taken into account; space will also be required for any youngsters which are bred. The exact layout of each birdroom very much depends on the requirements of the individual breeder. However, it is not usually a good idea to cram as many cages as possible into a birdroom. Space must be provided for work surfaces, storage and even a chair, so that you can rest a while in the company of your birds.

Lighting and Heating
Most birdrooms will benefit from the provision of electric lighting and in many cases this is essential. During the winter it is often impossible to undertake all the tasks necessary in maintaining a stud of exhibition birds during daylight hours.

On dull days it may be necessary to turn on the lights to supplement the normal levels of daylight. This is especially true in large, deep birdrooms, where very little light penetrates to the back except on the brightest of days. Having installed an electric supply to provide supplementary lighting, the provision of normal electric sockets for heaters and other electrical appliances would seem to be common sense. While canaries are not particularly susceptible to cold, it is wise to try and keep the minimum temperature in birdrooms just above freezing point. Electric heating which is thermostatically controlled tends to be most widely used for this purpose, as it is free from harmful fumes and easily maintained. Paraffin heaters and other forms of combustion heaters have caused countless disasters in birdrooms and canaries are particularly susceptible to toxic fumes. It is essential that an electric supply be correctly installed. Faulty wiring can result in fire or electrocution, neither of which are recommended.

Water Supply

It is a great advantage to have a properly plumbed-in sink and water supply in your birdroom. Obviously not all birdrooms can accommodate such a feature, but for the larger birdroom this will prove to be an invaluable asset. Not only will time be saved when giving birds fresh water, but the task of washing dirty pots, utensils, nest pans and show cages will be that much easier. Where a running water supply is to be installed, proper provision must be made for the disposal of dirty water. As this facility will be a 'one off' expense it is usually worthwhile to seek professional assistance, in order to avoid any unseen problems in the future.

Cages

Cages are usually constructed in blocks of doubles or trebles. However, each block of cages should not be so large that it cannot be easily moved for routine maintenance. Each block should be a self-contained unit and it is unwise to use the birdroom walls as the back of cages. This can lead to all sorts of problems, not least of which are difficulties in cleaning and repainting cages and the effective control and elimination of parasites which may infest cages from time to time. If blocks

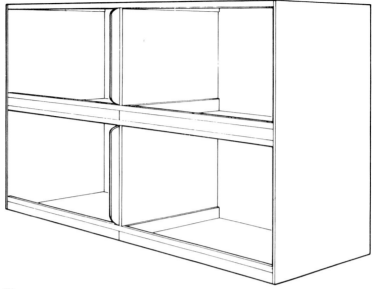

Fig. 3
A typical block of four breeding cages, shown with wire cage fronts removed.

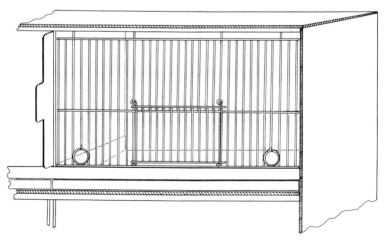

Fig. 4
A typical cage for housing canaries.

of cages are constructed as doubles, each cage should be about 2 ft (60 cm) in length with horizontally adjacent cages being divided by means of a removable slide. This permits each level to be converted into a 4 ft (1.2 m) flight cage as and when required. If these cages are made to about 12 in (30 cm) high and 15 in (38 cm) deep, each 2 ft (60 cm) cage can house one breeding pair of canaries.

Alternatively, with trebles, each cage will be about 16 in (40 cm) in length; removing dividing slides provides a 4 ft (1.2 m) flight cage, but only one breeding pair can be housed adequately on each tier. Usually trebles of this type will be about 12 in (30 cm) high and 12 in (30 cm) deep. The choice of cage depends on the owner. Doubles offer a more effective use of space for breeding, but trebles offer more space for housing birds individually during the show season. A block containing eight doubles will accommodate eight pairs and eight individual show birds. A block of twelve trebles will accommodate four breeding pairs and twelve individual show birds. A combination of both types of cages is probably ideal, provided sufficient room is available in the birdroom. Cages which have removable trays at the bottom allow for easier and more effective cleaning of cage floors.

All cages should be constructed from good quality plywood, with the sides, floors and tops being made from 3/8 in (9 mm) plywood and the backs and tray bottoms being 1/8 in (4 mm) plywood. Front rails are usually made from dressed softwood and should be about 1/2 in (12 mm) thick from back to front. Blocks of cages can be bought ready made, or constructed using a few basic carpentry skills. However, before making any cages it is advisable to obtain the wire fronts for them. It is much easier to build cages to meet the specification of the wire fronts than it is to modify the fronts to fit the cages. The type of wire fronts universally used for canaries are those which have headholes incorporated in the design. These allow the birds to be fed and watered by means of seed hoppers and glass-hat drinkers attached to the outside of the cage, and make the daily chores of feeding and watering that much quicker and easier to perform. When making the cages, ensure that the distance between the bottom of the top rail and the top of the bottom rail is about 1/2 in (12 mm) greater than the distance between the top and bottom horizontal wires of the cage front. This gives adequate room for the cage fronts to be fitted or removed without excessive bending of the wire front.

The vertical wires which extend above and below the top and bottom horizontal wires of the cage front are fixing wires. The usual method is to insert the top fixing wires fully into pre-drilled holes in the top front rail of the cage, and then insert the bottom fixing wires into a further set of pre-drilled holes in the top of the bottom front rail. When properly fitted the bottom horizontal wire should rest on the top of the bottom front rail. Should the front not fit easily and correctly, then the fixing wires may need to be slightly shortened. If you are in any doubt as to the best way to construct a block of cages, it is worth arranging to visit a few local fanciers, so that you can examine the style and construction of their cages. Most will be only too pleased to offer advice and warn of the difficulties and pitfalls they encountered when making their cages.

The wire fronts used for cages can be bought ready made in various standard sizes or made to your own personal requirements using punch bar and tinned wire. Cage fronts made from punch bar tend to be more serviceable and longer-lasting than spot-welded cage fronts. Punch bar which has holes set ⅝ in (16 mm) apart is the most suitable for canary cage fronts and can usually be bought to be used in conjunction with either 14-gauge or 16-gauge tinned wire, as preferred. Anyone who is reasonably adept at using a soldering iron should be able to make their own cage fronts with very little difficulty. The main priority is to make sure all the horizontal wires are parallel, and are at right angles to the vertical wires.

Painting

Once constructed, cages will need to be painted. All interior surfaces must be painted, as should the exterior surfaces of all front rails. Naturally, painting all the exterior surfaces will help to make the finished appearance that much better. Gloss paint is the most durable and relatively easy to clean. Silk vinyl paints are easier and quicker to apply, but are generally less hard-wearing than gloss paint. Cages painted with matt emulsion paints tend to absorb dirt and stains too easily and require repainting too frequently in order to keep them looking clean and tidy.

The choice of colour is really up to each individual breeder, but pale blue is favoured by many fanciers. Do not pick a colour which is too dark as this makes the birdroom look dingy.

Wire cage fronts must also be protected, as untreated wire soon rusts and becomes unsightly. Black stove enamel is most commonly used to provide an effective and hard-wearing protection for cage fronts. Whatever type of paint is used it is necessary to repaint cages and cage fronts on a regular basis in order to keep them clean and in good condition. Properly constructed cages and wire fronts will last for many, many years before needing to be replaced, provided they are cleaned, disinfected, repainted and repaired on a regular basis.

Perches

There are a wide variety of perches available for use in bird cages. Some are attached to the back of the cage, others twist on to the wire front, and others are braced between the back wall of the cage and the wire front. Twist-on perches are very popular, as they can be repositioned very easily and are quickly removed when cleaning is necessary. They do, however, tend to snap the vertical wires of spot-welded cage fronts and are perhaps best used in conjunction with cage fronts made from 14-gauge wire and punch bar. The usual diameter for perches is about ⅜ in (9 mm) and they should be made from softwood. They can be round, square or oval, and variations in perch diameter help the birds to keep their feet properly exercised and free from corns and other foot disorders.

Whatever style of perch is used, they must be kept clean by regular washing and disinfecting. Dirty perches are not just unsightly, they can be the breeding ground for various different organisms harmful to the birds and are particularly associated with eye infections. Perches must be securely fixed, so that they do not continually fall down, making the birds nervous. Never use frozen perches without first thawing them out thoroughly. If canaries roost on frozen perches this will often have fatal results.

Flight Cages and Aviaries

The use of indoor flight cages or aviaries can be extremely useful to the breeder of Gloster Canaries. Their primary function is to house young birds once they have been separated from their parents. A flight cage measuring about 7 ft (2.1 m) long, 3 ft (90 cm) high and 2½ ft (75 cm) deep can house up to 30 young Consorts or 25 young Coronas, and if this size flight cage is used, one can be positioned on top of the other to make a more economic use of space. Just as with breeding and stock cages, flight cages must be kept clean and properly decorated. Bigger flights can be used to house larger groups of Consorts, but Coronas are best kept in groups of no more than 25, in order to minimize the chances of excessive feather plucking. Damage to the plumage of the crest can effectively ruin the potential of exhibition stock.

Flight cages can also be used to provide additional exercise for flighted hens prior to the breeding season. Flight cages and flights are generally built around a timber framework, made to the size most suitable for the individual birdroom. Provision has to be made for doors to allow feeding and cleaning to be undertaken easily, and having taken these

Flight cages used to accommodate young Gloster Canaries after they have been removed from the care of their parents.

features into account, the framework can be covered with ½ in (12 mm) wire netting. Where one flight cage is positioned on top of another, the floors must be solid to prevent droppings falling from the top cage into the bottom one.

Outside garden aviaries can be very attractive features, but are not essential for the breeder of exhibition Gloster Canaries. Where outside aviaries are used care must be taken to ensure they are vermin-proof. If these aviaries allow birds access to the birdroom, any vermin entering the aviary will also have the opportunity to enter the birdroom. Aviary foundations must be properly sited and underground protection must be provided by placing ½ in (12 mm) wire netting around the whole perimeter of the aviary, from ground level down to 12 in (30 cm) below ground level. If cats or hawks may be a problem, double wire netting will need to be provided on all netted sections of the aviary. It is wise to have at least one side of the aviary completely enclosed and to have

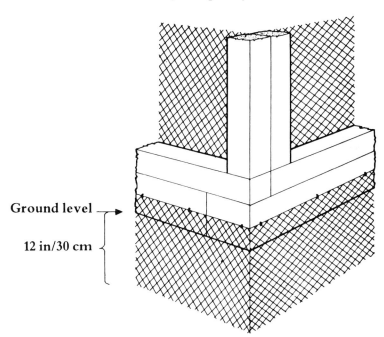

Ground level

12 in/30 cm

Fig. 5
Outdoor aviary section, showing positioning of wire netting below ground level.

49

at least part, if not all, of the roof covered with corrugated plastic sheets to give protection from inclement weather. Outdoor aviaries need regular maintenance: woodwork must be treated regularly with a suitable preservative, all wire sections must be checked for signs of damage or corrosion and aviary floors must be kept clean and tidy.

Initial Expenditure
It may seem to be a very costly business to house a stud of canaries properly. However, economies made with regard to the quality of materials used to construct a birdroom often result in excessive amounts of time being wasted during the day-to-day management of the stock maintained. It is always wise to provide birds with the best accommodation you can afford. Birds are only at their best when kept in good conditions and cannot be enjoyed unless they are happy and contented in their surroundings.

8   Feeding

The first essential with regard to feeding is that birds must always be provided with good-quality, clean, fresh food. The three basic constituents of a canary diet are seed, water and grit, and great care should be taken to ensure these are not deficient in any way. No amount of extras and additives can compensate for a poor basic diet.

Water
Canaries must always have access to clean, fresh water and it is important that this aspect of feeding is not neglected. Drinking water, for birds housed in cages, is usually provided either by means of 'glass-hat' drinkers or tubular plastic drinkers. While tubular drinkers tend to protect water from debris, such as sawdust, falling from other cages, they can also tempt fanciers not to provide fresh water on a daily basis. Glass-hat drinkers do not offer an opportunity to neglect this essential feature of canary management, as it is obvious to even the most inexperienced fancier that they will require daily attention. As well as discarding and replenishing

Various types of baths which can be used for canaries.

water on a daily basis, it is important that drinkers should also be kept clean and not be allowed to build up a layer of green algae on the inside surfaces. It is much easier to wash out and clean glass-hat drinkers on a regular basis than it is to keep tubular drinkers clean.

In addition to a constant supply of clean drinking water, canaries also appreciate being allowed to bathe regularly and baths should be provided as often as possible. For canaries it is most usual to provide the type of bath which can be attached to the cage front, allowing the birds access through the cage door. Various styles of these baths are generally available from pet shops; however the large style of bath with a plastic bottom and wire sides and top can also be used as a weaning cage during the breeding season.

Although some fanciers may advocate using only rain water for their birds, by far the safest and most convenient method is to use tap water. If there is any doubt over the purity of ordinary mains water then boiling it prior to use is probably the best remedy. As canaries must drink quite frequently their water supply can be used as a medium for providing medicines and tonics. Obviously when supplements are being administered in the drinking water, it would be foolish to provide baths as these offer the birds an alternative source of drinking water.

Hard Seed
Canaries will eat a wide selection of different seeds and most enjoy variety in their diet. Whatever seed is supplied, it must always be of good quality, Stale, dirty or tainted seed can only be detrimental to the health of the birds and will often be reflected in poor breeding results. For fanciers with a small stud it is foolish to buy large amounts of seed at one time, as the quality of seed deteriorates when stored over long periods. Buy seed from a reputable seed merchant, ordering only sufficient quantities to last about one month. Buying cheap seed can be one of the most expensive mistakes made by birdkeepers. It is unwise to store seed in air-tight containers, as this is detrimental to the condition of the seed and reduces its nutritional value. If you are in any doubt about the quality of a specific batch of seed it should not be used.

Canary Seed
This seed should form the basis of any diet for canaries and because it forms such a large part of the diet, it is essential that a good-quality canary seed is provided at all times. A good test of seed quality is to try sprouting a small amount on a sunny window sill. If the seed is kept moist it should begin to sprout within a few days. It is best to feed birds one specific type of canary seed rather than a mixture of different types. Where mixtures are provided, birds will often search their hoppers for a particular type of seed which they prefer. This results in the other types of seed being scattered from the hopper and consequently wasted. Canary seed is the only seed which can be safely given in excess to adult canaries.

Rape Seed
The seed most commonly used to supplement a basic diet of canary seed is rape. Three types of rape seed are generally available, these being black rape, red rape and rubsen rape. Black rape can tend to have a 'scouring' effect and upset the digestive system of canaries. Red rape is less stringent, but sometimes black rape which has been soaked in boiling water and then dried will be sold as red rape. Therefore unless you are sure the red rape provided is genuine, and not treated black rape, it can be a pointless exercise providing red rape. German rubsen rape is being favoured by an increasing number of fanciers at the present time as it is not too strong and is generally of a good quality. Rape seed is often mixed with canary seed and provided in hoppers as part of the basic seed diet. The usual ratio of the mixture is four parts of canary seed to one part rape, but if it is supplied in this manner it can lead to wastage due to birds searching hoppers for their favourite seed. Alternatively rape seed can be added to condition seed and given separately to the basic seed diet, about twice a week. Rape seed has a much higher fat content than canary seed and therefore should not be given in excessive amounts.

Niger Seed
Another seed with a high fat content is niger seed and this is also beneficial to canaries, provided it is not fed to excess. It is

most usually fed by adding it to a condition seed and is often recommended to prevent egg binding in hens. Niger seed is one of the first hard seeds to be eaten by young canaries once they have been weaned from their parents and is very useful in combating the problem of young birds going light. Great care must be taken to ensure that niger seed is fresh, as its condition deteriorates very quickly when it is stored incorrectly or in unsuitable conditions.

Hemp Seed
Adult canaries enjoy hemp seed in its whole form and this can also be added to a condition seed mixture. However, it should not be given in its whole form during the breeding season as it is a large seed and if fed directly to young birds it will block their digestive system. During the breeding season hemp is often fed in crushed form and small amounts are appreciated by feeding hens. Crushed hemp is particularly useful for young birds once they have been separated from their parents and are making the transition from rearing food to hard seed. It is wisest to buy whole hemp seeds and then make your own crushed hemp in small quantities, as and when required. This can be done using an ordinary household blender which is capable of grinding dry mixtures. Hemp also has a much higher fat content than canary seed.

Maw Seed
Another seed with a high fat content is maw seed, which is a very small, round, blue seed derived from a particular type of poppy. It is frequently found in condition seed mixtures and also regularly added to rearing food mixtures. Its presence in rearing food is said to encourage young canaries to peck at the small dark seeds and therefore it assists them to start feeding for themselves.

Linseed
Unfortunately some canaries are reluctant to eat this seed, which is of great benefit during the moult. Small amounts can be added to condition seed mixtures throughout the year and, provided birds are prepared to eat linseed, it can be increased during the moult.

Teazle
This is a very expensive seed and probably greatly over-valued.

Groats
Although not as popular with fanciers generally as they once were, groats are appreciated by most canaries and provide additional variety in their diet. Groats contain a high proportion of carbohydrates, have a similar nutritional content to that of canary seed and can prove to be an asset, especially during the breeding season.

Pinhead Oatmeal
This is often recommended by Gloster Canary breeders, but as the birds can cope with groats, from which pinhead oatmeal is derived, there seems to be little point in providing pinhead oatmeal.

Condition Seed
It is usually possible to buy ready-mixed condition seed, which contains many of the different seeds previously mentioned. This can be very convenient for fanciers with

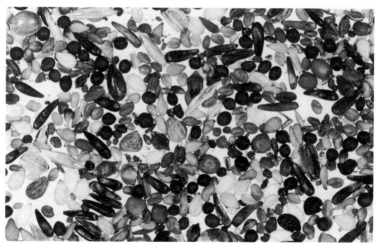

A typical condition seed mixture suitable for adult canaries, which would also be suitable for young birds if the larger types of seeds, such as hemp, were omitted from the mixture.

small studs of birds who probably find it is impractical to mix up a condition seed exactly to their requirements. Unless seed can be bought in very small quantities, it will have to be stored for long periods of time and therefore lose much of its nutritional value. Additionally many of the seeds used for condition seed mixtures have relatively poor keeping properties. However, for the fancier with a larger stud it is probably wisest to buy individual types of seed and then make a mixture which is suitable for the specific time of year it is to be used.

Screenings
Occasionally screenings, which are all the unwanted weed seeds collected at harvest time, can be obtained from farmers. Provided these have been properly stored and not treated with harmful chemicals, they are a very useful additive for condition seed mixtures.

Kraker Tonic Grains
This is a proprietary brand of seed mixture which contains many different seeds, most of which it would be impractical to buy individually. It can therefore be very useful in supplementing 'home-made' condition seed mixtures.

Kraker Tonic Grains as marketed by J. E. Haith Ltd.

Grit

Grit is essential for all canaries as it enables birds to grind the seed they eat so that it can be effectively digested. Hens coming into breeding condition must have access to adequate supplies of grit-based products in order to produce shells for the eggs they will lay. It is also important in providing small quantities of trace elements which are equally essential if birds are to remain fit and healthy. However, not all products sold as grit will be suitable for the needs of canaries and it is advisable to inspect supplies of grit regularly to ensure they will actually be of benefit to the birds. Occasionally mixtures containing very small smooth-edged pebbles are sold as grit. The smoothness of these pebbles makes them unsuitable for the primary function of grit, to grind seed. Grit should contain cut stone which has definite edges and corners which will grind seed effectively.

Mineralized Grit

The basic grit used by the majority of fanciers is generally referred to as mineralized grit. Not only should this grit contain the correct type of stones to grind seed, but it should also contain small amounts of vital trace elements.

A sample of the type of mineralized grit which is ideally suited to Gloster Fancy Canaries.

Limestone Grit

Small limestone grit is very often supplied in addition to mineralized grit prior to the breeding season in order to give hens adequate supplies of calcium for the purpose of egg-laying. As calcium is essential to promote healthy bone growth in developing embryos and chicks, it should not be forgotten that cock birds will also need to be given a source of additional calcium prior to the breeding season.

Oystershell Grit

This type of grit is supplied for the same reason as limestone grit and may be preferred by individual birds. As it is essential that birds have every opportunity to build up levels of calcium, there is no harm in providing oystershell grit, in addition to limestone grit, prior to the breeding season.

Charcoal

Charcoal is often added to supplies of grit before it is fed to birds. It is an aid to the digestive system and believed to absorb any impurities which may be by-products of the digestive system. Prior to the breeding season it is very important that birds should not be suffering from any digestive disorders, as these would be detrimental to their attempts to feed and rear healthy chicks. Charcoal should not, however, be given to excess, as not only does it absorb and effectively destroy impurities, but it can also absorb some vitamins, which are essential if good breeding results are to be achieved.

Rearing Food

In order to rear sound healthy baby canaries, it is almost certainly essential to provide parent birds and young birds not yet able to eat hard seed with some form of rearing food. Additionally rearing food is usually used as an aid to conditioning birds prior to the breeding season and to provide variety in the canaries' diet throughout the year. There are countless different rearing foods on the market, plus a great many more home-made preparations all of which can be used to assist in the rearing of young canaries. Whatever type of rearing food is used, it must not be allowed to remain in cages for more than 24 hours and all pots and

The ingredients for the preparation of rearing food.

Preparing chopped hard-boiled egg.

Adding a teaspoonful of glucose to the dry mixture.

containers should be washed out thoroughly each time they are used. A basic rearing food which has given good breeding results, in terms of both the number and the quality of young birds produced, is as follows:– 1 part Nectarblend, 1 part Haiths Condition and Rearing Food, 1 part sausage rusk, ¼ part maw seed, mixed thoroughly together and then made crumbly moist by gradually stirring in a little cold water. This produces the basic rearing food, which can be supplemented by various additives at the appropriate time.

Porridge
As a dietary supplement, when hens have youngsters to feed, a proprietary brand of oat flakes cereal can be added to the basic rearing food. The quantity added should be about one eighth of the total dry mixture used.

Hard-boiled Egg
Chopped hard-boiled egg has always been a reliable rearing food and even in this modern age of multivitamins and high-protein foods it is very hard to beat. It is probably best given alongside rearing food when hens have chicks to rear. This can be done by putting rearing food at one side of the egg drawer and hard-boiled egg at the other side.

Bread and Milk
As a change from the normal rearing food, wholemeal brown bread and milk can be offered to rearing hens occasionally in order to vary their diet. Each hen can be given a cube of bread moistened with a few drops of milk and sprinkled with maw seed. Indeed many birds have been reared using bread and milk as the sole rearing food. However, this is sometimes blamed for a high percentage of young birds 'going light' at about six to eight weeks of age. Naturally when using bread and milk great care must be taken to ensure it is not allowed to become sour.

Additional Conditioners
There are various other additives which are extremely valuable when used at the appropriate time. These are not necessarily nutritious in their own right but complement the diet given to birds.

Mixing rearing food to a crumbly consistency.

Rearing food being placed at one side of the egg drawer.

Chopped hard-boiled egg being placed at the opposite side.

Vitamin Powder

In order to ensure birds have adequate amounts of all the necessary vitamins required, multivitamin powders can be added to the rearing food prior to the breeding season and during the moult and also given to young birds which have been successfully weaned from their parents. It should not, however, be given to birds who are actually rearing, as this can make them overfit and cause them to desert their youngsters. If a vitamin powder such as SA37 is being used, one rounded teaspoonful of vitamin powder should be added to each pint of dry rearing food mixture, not including the maw seed. Ensure the powder is mixed thoroughly into the rearing food so that it is distributed evenly among all the birds to which it is given.

Cod Liver Oil

This is an excellent natural source of vitamins A and D, and can now be bought with added vitamin E. Vitamin D is essential prior to the breeding season. Unless birds have adequate levels of vitamin D they cannot absorb calcium into their systems. If hens cannot absorb sufficient calcium they are likely to lay eggs with poor shells which generally fail to hatch, or worse still they become egg-bound and will need to be rested for a considerable period before they can recommence breeding. Vitamin E is often called the fertility vitamin and may be destroyed by excessive levels of vitamin D. Therefore it would seem wise to use cod liver oil with added vitamin E. Probably the most effective method of adding cod liver oil to the diet is by incorporating it in the basic rearing food for about three months prior to pairing birds together. The quantity of cod liver oil required is one teaspoonful to each pint of rearing food, measured before the maw seed is added. The cod liver oil should then be mixed very thoroughly with the correct amount of maw seed required for the rearing food. Once the maw seed and cod liver have been mixed, they can be added to the dry rearing food and once again mixed in thoroughly. Water should then be added to produce the desired consistency. Cod liver oil can, of course, become rancid if not used carefully, but anyone who practises the basic rules of hygiene should not have cause for concern. Those who do not follow basic rules of hygiene will probably have run into serious trouble long before they start to use cod liver oil. All containers used to store food containing cod liver oil must be thoroughly washed after use. It is also advisable to buy a new bottle of cod liver oil at the beginning of each new season so that the strength of the product is assured.

Soluble Multivitamins
Soluble or liquid multivitamins can be useful in maintaining adequate levels of vitamins in stock prior to the breeding season and during the moult. At these times the recommended dose can be added to the drinking water twice a week. One of these which has proved particularly successful is Collovet, which can be obtained from most veterinary surgeons.

Glucose
This is an energy-giving supplement which can be added to the rearing food in the ratio of one rounded teaspoonful to each pint of dry rearing food mixture. It is particularly useful for young birds, after being weaned from their parents, and also for adult birds once they have completed their breeding season. It assists birds to cope with the moult, which can be a very stressful time of year.

Soaked Seed
Soaked seed is becoming increasingly popular with canary breeders and its main use is as a substitute for seeded chickweed during the breeding season. While it falls well short of chickweed as a rearing food, it can be very useful for breeders who are unable to collect seeded chickweed. Various mixtures which are suitable for canaries and soak easily are available from seed merchants. The seed needs to be soaked for about 24 hours and then rinsed thoroughly. Ideally it should be left to stand in a sieve for about 12 hours after soaking and rinsed again thoroughly before being added to the rearing food mixture. Soaked seed, once properly prepared, should be added to the dry rearing food in the ratio of one part soaked seed to two parts rearing food. However, it should not be offered to rearing hens until their young are at least 24 hours old. Soaked seed can also be used, as previously described, as a conditioning agent prior to the

breeding season. There is no need to sprout soaked seed before adding it to the rearing food and it is probably at its most beneficial just prior to sprouting.

Greenfood

Most canaries will enjoy a wide variety of greenfood. However, before any greenfood is fed to birds, fanciers must be sure it has not been contaminated by chemicals which could be harmful. When collecting greenfood from private land it is essential to ask permission from the owner and also find out if it has been treated in any way. As with other perishable foods, uneaten greenfood must be removed from cages and flights before it starts to decompose.

Chickweed *(Stellaria media)*

While it is not essential to feed chickweed during the breeding season, in its seeded form, it is one of the most useful rearing aids available to canary breeders. If you are able to collect seeded chickweed, this is a great advantage. It is pointless pulling the whole plant as the part of interest to canaries is the seed head and therefore it is necessary only to cut the top 4-5 in (10-12.5 cm). Although chickweed costs nothing in itself it can be a very expensive food when the time taken to gather it and the distances travelled to find it are taken into consideration. Ideally it should be fed in small bunches, seed heads uppermost, three or four times a day to all birds with young to feed.

Dandelion *(Taraxacum hamatum)*

Various parts of dandelion plants are fed by many canary breeders. The leaves are a good form of greenfood, unripened seed heads may be useful for rearing hens and the root is an excellent conditioner. However, dandelion is a powerful conditioner and when given to excess can make birds overfit. The root is an excellent pre-breeding season conditioner, but it is illegal in the UK under the terms of the Wildlife and Countryside Act to take the roots of any wild plant which is not growing on cultivated land. When roots are collected they can be washed and then grated to make them easier for the birds to eat, but be warned that dandelion root contains a very stubborn stain which is difficult to remove from clothes. Dandelion leaves will be appreciated in small amounts prior to breeding but should not be given to excess during the breeding season. Seeded dandelion heads, although enjoyed by some canaries, tend to fill the birdroom with dandelion fluff and are not as generally beneficial or as well received as seeded chickweed.

Green Vegetables
The leaves of many domestic green vegetables are enjoyed by most canaries. Greens are a good natural source of vitamins and trace elements and when fed in moderation will be of benefit to the birds' general health. A large cabbage leaf is often a useful diversion for groups of birds housed in flights or aviaries, and will tend to reduce squabbling.

Wild Seeds
The countryside produces a natural harvest of seeds, which are generally available from mid-summer through to mid-autumn. Many of these are extremely beneficial for birds provided they are not given to excess. Although wild seeds can help to maintain birds in good condition, none is absolutely essential to the development of a quality stud of canaries. When fed excessively, some wild seeds can produce a bronziness of colour and others may actually have the undesirable effect of colour feeding birds. It is impossible to mention every plant which provides seeds eaten by canaries, but a few of the more important plants and seeds are outlined here.

Seeding Grasses
The seed heads of wild grasses such as annual meadow grass *(Poa annua)*, Yorkshire fog *(Holcus lanatus)*, tufted hair-grass *(Deschampsia cespitosa)*, purple moor-grass *(Molinea caerulea)* and many more besides can be very useful for canary breeders. The light feathery nature of the seed heads often attracts the interest of young canaries and can help them to make a smooth transition from soft food to hard seed. Seeded grasses can also be used as a substitute for chickweed in the latter part of the breeding season, when adequate supplies of chickweed are generally very hard to find. The exact species of grass used is not important; it is the style of the grass

which matters. Grasses with very small seeds and delicate seed heads are to be preferred; those with larger seeds such as ryegrass tend to be less popular.

Greater Plantain *(Plantago major)*

The seed spikes of greater plaintains or 'rats tails' are greatly enjoyed by canaries and will be appreciated both in their unripened and ripened forms. They are especially beneficial for birds during the moult, but if stored can also be fed throughout the autumn and winter. When collecting seed heads for storing, choose ones that are ripe and not in their green form. Once gathered, they can be tied in bunches and hung up to dry. They should not be stored in damp or stuffy conditions, as this will cause them to become mouldy.

Sea Arrow Grass *(Triglochin maritimum)*

Anyone living within easy reach of salt marshes should be able to find an abundant supply of seeded sea arrow grass from midsummer to early autumn. This 'grass' has seed spikes, which on initial examination resemble those of the greater plantain. However, the individual seed capsules are set slightly further apart than those of the greater plantain, and each capsule contains several flat, disc-shaped seeds greatly appreciated by canaries. Seed spikes of the sea arrow grass can also be stored and used later in the year.

Redshank or Persicaria *(Polygonum persicaria)*

This plant produces a seed which is very beneficial to canaries, especially during the moult. A characteristic of the plant is that the leaves usually have a dark spot in the centre. Generally it has clusters of small pink flowers which contain black disc-shaped seeds. It is often found growing profusely on agricultural land such as potato fields, but if you are collecting from such areas it is imperative to consult the land owner to ensure it has not been treated with harmful chemicals.

Knotgrass *(Polygonum aviculare)*

A close relative of redshank is knotgrass, and this also provides a seed which is useful during the moult. It is not a true grass and tends to be a low creeping plant with small pink flowers along the stem. As soon as the plant flowers, it contains a seed and therefore it can usually be fed by early summer. Unfortunately it is very prone to mildew and should not be collected if suffering from this condition.

Meadow Sweet or Queen of the Meadows
(Filipendula ulmaria)
This is another plant which provides seed which is especially beneficial to canaries during the moult. It tends to grow in damp places and has quite twiggy stems topped with dense clusters of white flowers. The seeds are contained in small green spheres and the plant is usually in seed throughout the summer months.

Dock Family (Polygonaceae)
The dock family includes such plants as redshank and knotgrass, which have been mentioned specifically. It also includes members of the *Rumex* genus, all of which provide seed, especially in its unripened form, which will be appreciated by canaries. Once the seed ripens and the seed heads become brown most canaries will lose interest. Members of the dock family are useful because they tend to produce usable seed relatively early in the year.

Cabbage Family (Cruciferae)
Many members of the cabbage family produce seeds which have been widely used for feeding canaries. These include black mustard, wild cabbage, turnip, white mustard and charlock, all of which have seed very similar to rape, which is also a member of the cabbage family.

Goosefoot Family (Chenopodiaceae)
This family of plants also contains many members which produce seeds appreciated by canaries. Suitable sources of seeds include various forms of goosefoot and orache, fat hen and even sugar beet, which when seeded will provide a little extra variety to the basic diet.

Practical Considerations
Although canaries will eat a wide variety of foods, it is neither possible nor advisable to include every food mentioned

in this chapter in their diet. Breeders should work out a sensible diet which provides the birds with all the essential nutrients they require without being excessive. It is quite possible to have too much of a good thing. Fanciers should also be realistic and choose a diet that can actually be maintained while still leaving time to enjoy the birds. There is little point deciding to use chickweed if you do not have sufficient sources or opportunities to collect adequate quantities; on the other hand, if ample supplies of chickweed are available, it is probably a waste of time providing soaked seed.

9 General Management

Even if you have obtained good-quality birds, fed them a properly balanced diet, and housed them in a well-designed birdroom, your chances of success will be minimal unless you also employ good general management techniques throughout the year.

Cages and Flights

Cages and flights used to house birds must be cleaned out regularly and it is advisable to make this a regular weekly job. If they are not cleaned out on a weekly basis, then general management is less then perfect. Various materials such as sawdust, sand or cat litter may be used as a floor covering, but generally sawdust is most commonly used, being ideal for breeders of exhibition birds. The sawdust used should be derived from untreated softwood timber and of as coarse a grade as possible. Hardwood sawdust tends to be too fine, causing eye trouble and respiratory disorders in stock. If you are in any doubt as to the suitability of sawdust, either with regard to its cleanliness or its composition, it should not be used.

Old sawdust, or other floor coverings, must be removed during cleaning. Removable cage trays and flight floors should be scraped clean where necessary, before being liberally re-covered with clean sawdust. Dirty cages are ideal places for breeding germs, bacteria and parasites, but very much less ideal for attempting to breed birds. Experienced fanciers may develop a few 'dodges' whereby they clean cages less frequently than once a week, but in truth they are only fooling themselves. Newcomers who are not prepared to spend the time and effort required in cleaning their cages once a week cannot expect to be successful and should perhaps consider a less demanding hobby.

In addition to the weekly cleaning routine, blocks of cages need to be washed out thoroughly twice a year. The most usual times to do this are at the end of the show season and the end of the breeding season. Washing cages is easier if you use a liquid biological detergent as a cleaning agent. The cages must not only be clean, they must also be disinfected, any common household disinfectant, diluted appropriately, being quite suitable for this purpose. After washing and disinfecting, cages should be sprayed with Ban Mite, which is a malathion-based preparation which will help to destroy these most troublesome creatures. At the same time as cages are being washed, wire cage fronts will also need to be cleaned, and if necessary, repaired and repainted.

If cages are gloss painted they will need a fresh coat of paint about once every four years. If silk-finish emulsion is used, then repainting will be required at least once every other year, while matt emulsion paint usually needs repainting annually.

Perches
Ensuring that perches are clean is just as important as making sure cages are clean. Perches should be soaked in a solution of biological detergent and disinfectant until clean, wiped with a clean cloth and rinsed thoroughly in clean water before being replaced. When perches are damp it is essential during cold weather to ensure that they cannot be frozen. If canaries roost on damp frozen perches, including natural perches collected during winter, this can often prove fatal. Obviously it is advantageous if two sets of perches are available, allowing each set to be cleaned and dried thoroughly before being reused. The use of dirty perches often leads to eye and foot disorders in stock. Perches which fit badly and continually fall down serve only to make stock nervous and flighty.

Drinkers
Canary breeders will generally find it advisable to use glass-hat drinkers, rather than tubular plastic drinkers, as the former demand regular daily attention. Birds should be provided with fresh water daily, and in hot weather twice daily and drinkers should be rinsed out every day. This rinsing can be made more effective by the addition of an

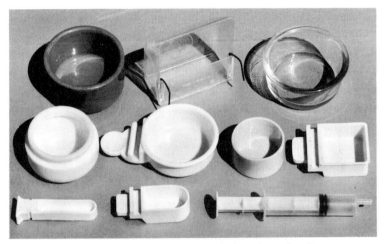

A sample of the different food and water pots which can be used in the management of canaries.

iodine-based disinfectant to the rinse water. Additionally drinkers should be placed in a solution of bleach for about 30 minutes each week, and then rinsed thoroughly in clean water before being replaced on stock cages and refilled. Allowing green algae to build up on inside surfaces of drinkers is inexcusable and not consistent with good management. Lazy breeders may claim that this algae provides trace elements, but if the birds require trace elements, there are numerous preparations commercially available which can provide them without risking the health of your stock. Water is an excellent breeding ground for many organisms which spread disease. Failure to pay proper attention to the provision of fresh water in clean drinkers is 'flying in the face of adversity'.

Food

In providing a diet of good-quality canary seed, seed hoppers need to be removed from cages, have the loose husks blown from the top of the seed and be topped with fresh canary seed daily. Additionally all seed in hoppers should be sieved once a week, usually after cleaning out the cages, to remove particles of dust which collect in the hoppers. All pots used to supply rearing food must be removed within 12 hours of

71

Various styles of seed and water hoppers which can be used for canaries.

being placed in cages, and then thoroughly washed ready for the next time they are required. If grit and condition seed is supplied simply by scattering adequate amounts on the cage floor, then there will be no need to clean and wash out grit pots or fingerdrawers. However, fanciers employing this time-saving method must ensure that their cages are cleaned out once a week, otherwise birds will be picking up not only grit or condition seed from the cage floor, but also disease and infection.

The Birdroom
As well as being well constructed and tidy the birdroom must also be properly maintained throughout the year. In the case of timber structures, this will mean treating all exterior surfaces with wood preservative annually. The interior birdroom floor should also be treated with a preservative to prevent any rot developing.

When maintaining a stud of canaries it is impossible to keep the floor of the birdroom dry as the birds will require regular baths and frequent spraying. Creosote is quite suitable as an interior preservative and will ensure the floor is fully protected. Naturally, when the floor is being treated, it is most important that the birdroom is adequately ventilated to prevent the build-up of any fumes which may be harmful to the birds. Adequate ventilation should not be a problem as birdrooms suitable for canaries must include in their design a good ventilation system. Creosote is equally suitable as a wood preservative for outside surfaces, but tends to be rather dark and unsightly. Many people prefer to use a preservative of a lighter colour, despite the additional expense, simply because the finished result is more attractive.

The roof of the birdroom will require inspection to ensure that it is sound and weatherproof and any necessary repairs should be carried out as soon as possible. Gutters and drainage systems must also be kept clean and in good repair, ensuring they function properly. A little regular maintenance is much to be preferred, rather than infrequent major structural repairs.

Birds
While the fancier is busy making sure that all the hardware used in birdkeeping is in perfect order, he or she should not forget to observe each individual bird on a daily basis. All birds should be kept clean and this may mean that some birds will require specific attention. Birds with dirty feet or soiled vents need to be caught and cleaned. When cleaning birds, soak the soiled areas gently in warm water until the dirt is loosened sufficiently to be removed without any discomfort to the bird. Roughness and impatience when handling birds will be detrimental to their condition and confidence.

Canaries must be dusted with mite powder both before and after breeding to ensure that stock does not become infested with red mite or northern mite. Usually birds will need to be dusted on three separate occasions prior to the breeding season and twice after the breeding season. Should an outbreak of mite occur, then additional dusting will be necessary for all infested birds and also all birds which have recently been in contact with these individuals. Northern mite is particularly difficult to eradicate from birdrooms once it has become established. A careful watch should be kept for any birds indulging in excessive preening or for very tiny black specks of swarming mite on cage walls and in nests.

Useful Gadgets

As time passes birdkeepers will build up an array of useful gadgets which help them to perform routine management tasks more efficiently. The blade from an old box plane will prove invaluable: it can be a wide scraper for cage floors or a narrow scraper for corners; the hole in the centre is ideal for scraping perches; the blade can be used for cutting and it can even be used as a hammer. A pair of half-rounded scissors is another very useful item in the birdroom, being ideal for vent trimming and nest trimming. For the larger stud, a trolley to carry food and food pots will save time when feeding the birds. Additionally it is worth remembering to include some seating arrangements in your birdroom so that you can sit in comfort and simply enjoy watching the birds.

Routine

All birdkeepers find it very useful to adopt a set routine when managing their stock, as this makes mistakes much less likely to occur. If birds are fed and watered in a haphazard manner it is very easy to miss a cage. Try and keep drinkers and seed hoppers in the same position on each cage, use identity cards or markers to indicate which birds require rearing food during the breeding season and perform weekly tasks on specific days so that they are not inadvertently overlooked.

The task of feeding birds and the day-to-day general management of the stud during the breeding season must be undertaken in an orderly manner.

10 Breeding

In order to establish a successful stud of Gloster Canaries it is essential to breed fit, healthy canaries from your stock. An inability to master the art of canary breeding will inevitably place anyone hoping to own top-quality exhibition specimens in an impossible situation. Obtaining good breeding results is very much dependent on preparing stock birds properly before commencing to pair them together. No matter how skilful the breeder, it is often impossible to rectify mistakes made prior to the breeding season once birds have been mated together.

Preparation

While canaries can be 'forced' into breeding condition with the use of artificial light and heat, beginners will usually be much more successful if they attempt to breed from their birds at the natural time of year. This means that feeding and management should be geared to pairing birds together in spring-time, and if they are a little backward with regard to condition, then waiting a while longer will do no harm. In addition to conditioning birds properly, all items of equipment used during the breeding season, including cages, should be made ready so that they are in first-class order in anticipation of their use.

The usual time to start conditioning canaries is in mid-winter and at this time, in addition to their basic seed mixture, they should be receiving rearing food, condition seed and additional supplies of grit, including limestone and oyster-shell grit plus a little charcoal. The rearing food provided to promote breeding condition should be supplemented with cod liver oil and also a vitamin powder such as SA37; all birds should be provided with about one teaspoonful of this food twice a week for three months prior to breeding. Condition

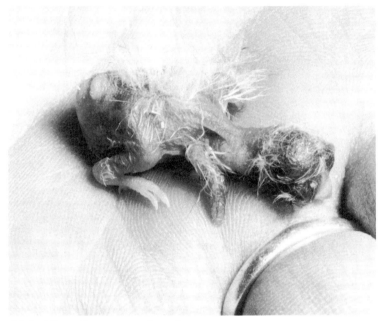

A baby Gloster Canary at two days of age.

seed can also be given twice a week in just sufficient quantities to ensure it is all eaten within twelve hours. If birds are receiving a staple diet of plain canary seed at this time, the condition seed mixture should include rubsen rape, niger seed and a tonic seed, such as Kraker Tonic Grains, plus a little hemp and groats. Fresh grit must also be given twice a week, this being scattered on cage floors, in small enough quantities not to create excessive waste. As an additional conditioner a liquid multivitamin preparation, such as Collovet, can be added to the drinking water once a week.

Hens should be given as much exercise as possible during this period and will generally be housed in small groups, either in double breeders (approx. 4 ft/1.2 m in length) or in flights, should these be available. During the three months prior to the breeding season it is wise to dust all birds with an effective mite powder on three separate occasions. The final treatment should only be a light dusting about three weeks before pairing birds together. While birds are being handled,

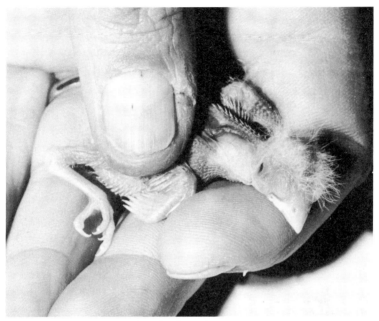

A young Gloster Canary at about five days of age.

their claws should be examined and any overgrown nails can be trimmed using a small pair of sharp scissors. Take care not to trim too close to the central blood vessel, otherwise bleeding will result. Many breeders will also take this opportunity to trim the vent feathers, as it is believed to improve the chances of effective mating. There is, however, no need to give the birds a 'short back and sides': it is sufficient just to trim lightly the ends of the top layer of feathers covering the vent.

Cages will all have been thoroughly washed out, sprayed with Ban Mite and, where necessary, repainted. Fixing hooks for nest pans also require checking to make sure they are safe and secure. If fanciers have prudently decided to fasten nest pans by means of a bolt and wing nut, then the bolts must be serviced by painting them thoroughly with light engineering oil and checking that the wing nut can be tightened and untightened easily. Should the wing nut not travel freely and easily, oil the bolt again until movement is satisfactory. Nest felts will need to be purchased and thoroughly treated with mite powder before being sewn into nest pans in readiness for the breeding season. When treating nest felts it is advisable to wear a protective mask to prevent inhalation of the powder, as the nest felts need to be well impregnated with mite powder and this is bound to create a dusty atmosphere. Preparation of nest felts and nest pans should be carried out well away from any food sources to prevent accidental contamination. For Gloster Canaries it is advisable to use small nest pans rather than large ones, at least until youngsters are about seven days old. As they are a small breed, satisfactory incubation is more likely in a snug nest pan. Larger nest pans can be used to replace small ones which contain larger babies and have become rather overcrowded.

A supply of nesting material will also be required. This should consist of fine dry grass and moss. It is perhaps unwise to treat nesting material with mite powder as this could accidentally be ingested by the birds during nest building. However, if the nesting material is collected a month prior to the breeding season and kept isolated from the birds, any parasites which affect birds should have been 'starved' by the time the nesting material is actually used. Nesting material must be dried naturally and stored in such a way that air is able to circulate freely through the material, in net bags for example, until it is required.

Egg boxes, which are used to store eggs prior to incubation, must also be checked to ensure they are in good order. They must be properly labelled, so that eggs which have been removed cannot accidentally become mixed up with those of other hens laying at the same time. It is a good idea to make the layout of the compartments in the egg box match the layout of the breeding cages so that it is obvious which eggs came from which cage. If breeding cages are constructed in blocks of eight, and there are two blocks side by side, then the egg box should have sixteen separate compartments and be numbered to correspond with the breeding cages. Each compartment needs to be large enough for eggs to be removed from the egg box without any danger of cracking. They also need to be lined with soft material such as clean, soft, white sawdust. A supply of dummy eggs will also be required. These are used as substitutes for the first three eggs in each clutch, which are then returned to the

A well-ordered egg box, correctly numbered, used for storing eggs prior to incubation.

nest once the fourth egg is laid. This procedure ensures that the chicks in each clutch hatch as near the same time as possible, and therefore allows the best chance of the full clutch being successfully reared.

All breeding record books and cards should be prepared prior to the breeding season. It is important to know the exact parentage of all young produced if they are to be used in future breeding programmes. Usually this means keeping a record book, which details each specific pairing and all the young produced from that pairing. However, cage record cards attached to each cage are also very useful to keep a check on the day-to-day progress of each pair. Also required will be a supply of numbered rings which can be used to identify each individual youngster produced.

Assessing Breeding Fitness

For the beginner it can be very difficult to assess the breeding fitness of birds. Even experienced fanciers can be misled into thinking their birds are fit enough to pair together, when in fact they are not. Pairing up too early is a far more serious problem than pairing up too late. Remember that cock birds 'tell lies': they will sing and sing, well before they are actually ready to be mated to the hens. Breeding readiness should be assessed by the condition of the hens. They will start to carry small pieces of material in their beaks as breeding time approaches, but often they will do this a full month before they are actually ready to 'go down'. As their condition improves many will be seen trying to pull feathers from their breasts in order to start building and they will be continually 'calling' to cock birds. The atmosphere in the birdroom will become more and more intense as the condition of the birds improves, until it is almost 'electric' and becomes what can only be described as a 'hive of activity'. Not until this situation is reached can canaries be expected to breed successfully.

Pairing
Once birds have attained the necessary level of condition, cages can be prepared for 'action'. Each pair should be allocated its own breeding cage, which, in addition to the normal seed and water, should contain an ample supply of

A nest pan with a sitting hen. Note the square of Perspex positioned between the nest pan and the cage wall to prevent excessive soiling of the cage wall when youngsters hatch.

grit, a scattering of condition seed, a few pieces of chick-weed, two perches, a nest pan complete with nest felt and a small amount of nesting material. When the nest pan is positioned in the cage it is advisable to fix a thin piece of Perspex, or other suitable material, about 5 in (12.5 cm) square, in between the nest pan and the cage wall. This will help to prevent the cage wall near to the nest pan becoming heavily soiled during the breeding season and therefore make the task of washing out cages later in the year much easier. Provided conditioning has been done correctly and the birds have not been paired together too soon, pairs should settle quickly and there will be very little fighting between cocks and hens. On very rare occasions two totally incompatible birds are selected as mates, and the only answer is to select new mates for these birds. If one cock bird is mated to more than one hen, he will have to spend time with each partner and should be transferred from breeding cage to breeding cage three or four times each day until eggs are laid.

Nest Building and Egg Laying
As hens start to build they will require additional supplies of nesting material. Some will prefer to build in a different site to the one chosen by their owner. In these cases the nest pan can be temporarily placed on the floor of the cage, in the position the hen has chosen until she lays and begins sitting. At this time the nest pan can be moved back to the position preferred by the birdkeeper and in the majority of cases the hen will accept the situation and continue incubation. Normally hens lay their first egg seven days after pairing, but of course there are variations. Some hens may lay one or two 'rogue' eggs virtually as soon as they are mated. Provided preparation and diet have been correct, this will cause no problem and these eggs can be discarded immediately. However, eggs laid as soon as four days after pairing can be fertile, and these should not automatically be discarded. Naturally other hens will take a little longer to lay, but all should have started to lay within fourteen days of pairing.

Once the first egg is laid it should be removed from the nest and placed in the egg box. The hen can then be given a dummy egg as a replacement. Dummy eggs can be used as replacements on a daily basis, but in a large stud it will be more convenient to replace the first egg with two dummy eggs and then no more additional dummy eggs will be required until it is time to replace the real eggs. Hens should have their real eggs returned on the morning that the fourth egg is laid and the incubation period is counted from this time. Should any eggs produced be dirty or soiled, it may be possible to clean them with a damp tissue if you are very careful. However, it is better to have dirty eggs than cracked eggs.

When the proper clutch of eggs is replaced this is a good opportunity to tidy up and rebuild any poor nests. Dry grass can be fashioned into a nest shape and placed in the nest pan. It should then be compressed, using the bottom of a jam jar to maintain the shape, and then it can be lined using kapok or some similar soft material. Finally any untidy pieces of grass can be trimmed off using scissors, before the nest, complete with eggs, is returned to the hen. Indeed fanciers may prefer to carry out this procedure on all nests, safe in the knowledge that they will then all be constructed satisfactorily. If nest pans are fastened inside the cage using a wing nut and bolt, the nest should be covered with a piece of felt until the wing nut is securely in place. It is just possible that you will drop the wing nut and if you have not taken adequate precautions, you can bet it will fall into the nest and break every egg in the clutch.

Exactly how many eggs will be laid in each clutch depends very much on the individual birds, but can also be affected by diet. Birds which have received adequate supplies of rearing food prior to the breeding season should lay four or five eggs without any problem. The usual incubation period for a canary egg is 13 or 14 days, but can vary from nest to nest. When eggs are returned, the cage record card should be appropriately marked so that the breeder knows that the cage contains a sitting hen and the date the eggs are due to hatch. During the incubation period hens will appreciate being

(photos opposite) An untidy and badly constructed nest can be rebuilt. After removing the eggs to a safe place, a suitable glass jar can be used to shape the cup of the nest, which should be lined with kapok. A final trim will improve the appearance of the nest and greatly reduce the chances of mishaps during the incubation period. Once this has been done the eggs can be replaced and the hen allowed to recommence sitting.

sprayed gently with water twice a week, as long as you take care not to get the nest too wet. Their diet can be limited to plain canary seed and water while they are sitting.

Hatching

The day before eggs are due to hatch, cage record cards should be amended to show that the arrival of youngsters is imminent. The young may hatch more easily if the eggs are lightly sprayed with warm water at this time, and this spraying also permits the nests to be checked a day early just to make sure youngsters have not hatched sooner than expected. While the normal incubation period is 13 or 14 days, some eggs may take up to 16 days to hatch.

If eggs have not hatched after 16 days' incubation they should be candled to check for fertility. This involves viewing the egg while it is being held in front of a reasonably bright light source. If the egg is fertile, the developing embryo will be seen as a dark area inside the egg through which light cannot pass. If the egg appears clear inside and there is no evidence of an embryo forming, then it is infertile

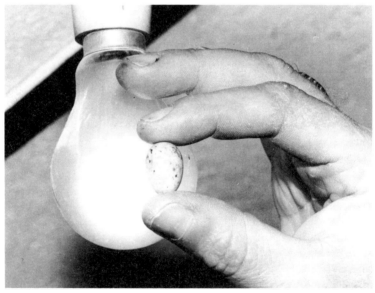

An illustration of the procedure for candling eggs by examining them against a light source, in order to check fertility.

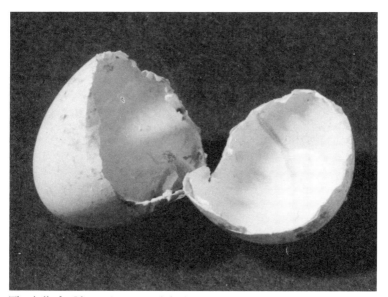

The shell of a Gloster Canary egg left after a good clean hatch.

and will never hatch. Clear eggs can be discarded immediately, unless the hen is required as a foster parent, but full eggs, those which contain an embryo, should be replaced and incubation allowed to continue for a further two days. Where eggs have failed to hatch after 18 full days of incubation, they can be discarded and the nest removed for a few days before being replaced to allow the hen to lay a new clutch of eggs. In the majority of cases, given good preparation, the eggs will hatch normally on the fourteenth or fifteenth day of incubation. As soon as young have hatched, cage record cards should be marked to show this fact and the management of the birds can be suitably amended.

Standard Procedure

As soon as young hatch, an egg drawer containing half a teaspoonful of basic rearing food and half a teaspoonful of chopped hard-boiled egg should be placed in the breeding cage, together with a sprig of seeded chickweed. Ideally, once these have been provided, the hen will leave the nest in order to feed and when she returns to the nest she will in turn feed her babies. As the young grow, the amounts of food

Serving rearing food, chopped hard-boiled egg and chickweed during the breeding season.

A nest containing recently hatched Gloster Canary chicks.

86

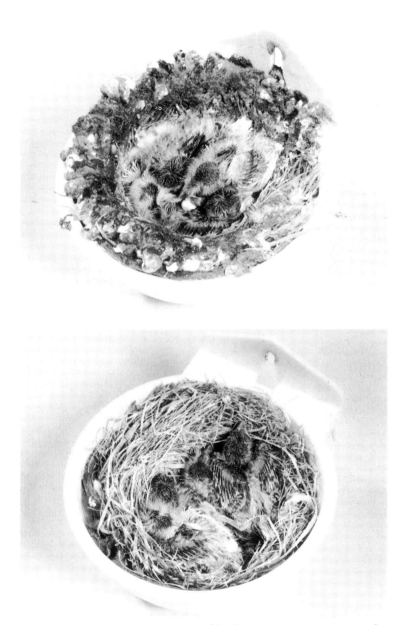

As nests become dirty due to the presence of developing youngsters, a new nest plan and clean nesting material can be provided to minimize the risk of disease and infection.

A young Corona and Consort still in the nest at about 16 days of age.

supplied will need to be increased and, if possible, fresh food should be provided four or five times each day. Nests containing youngsters should be checked twice a day to make sure all is well and cage floors should be inspected carefully in case any youngsters have fallen from the nest. If this occurs, even though the young chick seems very cold, it will very often revive if warmed up in your hands and breathed on gently for about five or ten minutes. Once the warmth has revived the youngster it can be placed back in its nest. After handling youngsters it is a wise precaution to wash your hands before any other youngsters are handled as this will prevent the possible spread of bacteria from one nest to another.

Gloster Canary breeders should be looking for nests containing three or four youngsters. If fewer than three youngsters hatch, parent birds can have insufficient rearing duties to keep them occupied and they tend to neglect the youngsters. More than four youngsters in one nest is really too much of a burden on most parent birds and usually results in the youngsters not being properly fed. Nests and nest pans are bound to become dirty and soiled if they

contain healthy young canaries and when they do the dirty
nest pan should be replaced with a clean one, once again
containing dry grass and kapok fashioned into a tidy nest.
Youngsters should grow well provided they are being
properly fed by their parents. By the time they are 14 days
old they will be feathering up nicely and at 21 days most will
have just left the nest. However, it is essential that Gloster
Canary breeders realize that young Glosters will only rarely
be able to feed themselves at 21 days old, despite the fact that
other breeds of canaries can often be taken from their parents
at this age. Generally speaking, Glosters cannot be weaned
from their parents until 25 or 26 days of age, and some may
take even longer.

Ringing

At some point youngsters will need to be 'marked' so that
their parentage will be known later in the year. For this
purpose fanciers can either use closed rings or split rings. If
closed rings are used the young will need to be rung as soon
as they start to excrete droppings over the side of the nest and
the hen is no longer cleaning the nest. Close-ringing birds
can seem to be a tricky operation, but once the technique is
mastered it is quite straightforward. The ring is slid over the
three forward-pointing toes on to the ball of the foot and
then drawn up the leg and over the back claw to the knee
joint; at this point the back claw can be eased free from under
the ring and the task is complete. Provided canaries are rung
at the correct age there should be no problems with regard to
parents rejecting close-rung babies.

However, it is not necessary to close-ring Gloster Canaries
at the present time; split-ringing is perfectly acceptable and
these rings can be put on any birds at any time. Some canaries

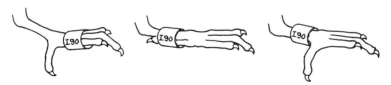

Fig. 6
Close-ringing a canary chick.

A young Gloster Corona Canary at eight days of age; this is about the right size for close-ringing, should this policy be adopted.

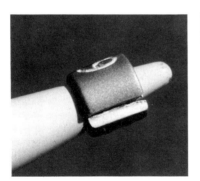 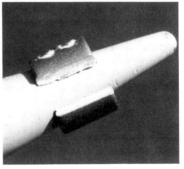

By placing the metal split ring on the tip of a knitting needle, a metal split ring can be opened sufficiently to allow it to be placed on a bird to be rung.

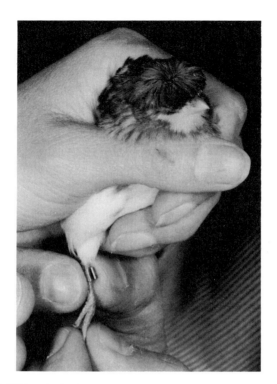

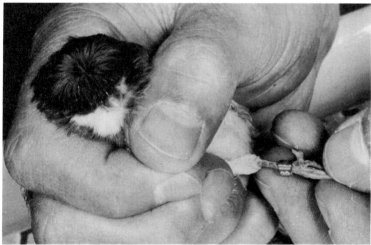

Attaching a metal split ring to the leg of a bird; firm but careful and gentle pressure on the ring is sufficient to close the ring.

are particularly adept at removing split plastic rings and therefore it is wisest to use split metal rings. These can be opened by sliding the ring on to the point of a ⅛ in (4 mm) diameter knitting needle until it is opened sufficiently to be placed on the leg of young birds. The ring can then be carefully closed simply by firm fingertip pressure.

Whatever form of ring is used, birds must be marked before they are separated from their parents and details of the ring worn by the bird and its parents must be recorded accurately. Both closed and split metal rings are available from the International Gloster Breeders Association, or can be obtained directly from ring manufacturers.

Weaning
The weaning procedure for Gloster Canaries should start when birds are about 18 days old. The nest pan containing the youngsters should be placed on the cage floor, not too close to the cage walls, as this will lead to the cage becoming soiled. At this time the cage should be thoroughly cleaned, washed and disinfected to minimize any risk of infections and disease in the next round of young. This having been done a fresh nest pan, properly prepared, can be placed in the original nesting site ready for the next clutch of eggs.

Young Coronas housed in flight cages after being separated from their parents.

Young Glosters being accommodated in a large wire bath while their parents are allowed to begin their second round. The young can still be fed by their parents through the cage wires.

Lowering the nest pan when the young are 18 days old increases the chances of them remaining in their own nest and not simply taking over the new nest pan. Ideally, if the cock has been left with the hen, he will be attending to the majority of the feeding duties, allowing the hen to concentrate on her next clutch of eggs. Unfortunately, cock birds can be less than perfect parents and the hen may have to feed the youngsters as well as starting her second clutch.

Should the young become a nuisance or start being used as nesting material by the hen, they can be separated from the parent birds by means of a wire slide. This will allow the youngsters to be fed while reducing the interference they may cause and the chances of feather plucking. If it is not possible to subdivide the breeding cage by means of a wire slide, a large wire bath can be used to house the youngsters. This should be fitted with a single perch situated as near to the closed end of the bath as is practical. If the perch is too close to the cage front, parent birds may be able to pull out the tail feathers of their young through the bars of the cage. While this may not matter with some breeds of canary it is very important that Gloster Canaries do not lose their tails when unflighted birds, as this will have the effect of increasing their overall length and therefore reduce their chances on the show bench.

While the young are being separated from their parents they can also be given their own supply of rearing food and chickweed, enabling them to start feeding for themselves. Once youngsters are eating food properly they can be transferred to indoor flight cages. Coronas should be parted from Consorts at this age, with birds being housed in groups of up to 25 or 30. If Consorts are not kept separate from Coronas, it will often lead to young Coronas having their crests plucked, and this should be avoided. Before the young birds are transferred to flight cages they must be rung and details of the ring fitted and each birds' parentage entered in the breeding records. If separated young begin to cry for food they should be transferred back to their parents for a few more days.

After-care

Once young have been successfully housed in groups they will require a diet of basic rearing food with added glucose and SA37 supplied fresh twice daily, crushed hemp supplied fresh every day, and a seed mixture of 65 per cent niger seed, 25 per cent rubsen rape and 10 per cent black rape, lightly sprinkled with plain canary seed. As time passes the amount of canary seed in the mixture will be increased gradually and by the time the young are about ten weeks old the mixture will contain 50 per cent canary seed. Young canaries need daily access to fresh rearing food until they are fully through the moult.

Trouble-shooting

When trying to breed from any type of livestock all sorts of complications can arise, and Gloster Canaries are no exception to this rule. There are countless problems which can arise during any breeding season; some can be overcome but others cannot. Each individual problem can be caused by a variety of factors and may respond to only one of a number of possible solutions. Outlining some of the commoner faults and the most likely solutions may help the beginner to overcome some of the setbacks which may be encountered.

Infertility

There are many reasons for birds producing infertile eggs, but the most common reason is poor preparation by the breeder. Once eggs have been incubated for seven days they can be candled to see if they are fertile. Before deciding to do this the breeder must be confident that he or she can handle eggs without damaging them and can recognize the difference between fertile eggs and infertile eggs.

What to do once eggs are found to be infertile is largely a matter of personal preference. Many canary breeders prefer to allow hens to sit out their full incubation period whether or not the eggs are fertile. In a large stud, a few hens with infertile eggs may be an asset, as they can be used as foster parents for chicks which are not being properly fed by their natural mothers. In a small stud, a few hens with infertile eggs can account for a large proportion of the breeding stock and therefore the breeder may prefer not to keep all of these birds sitting on clear eggs.

There may be some good reasons for allowing hens to sit out their full incubation period, but this is not strictly necessary. Once the breeder is confident that the eggs are infertile the nest can be removed for a couple of days and then replaced to allow the hen and her mate to produce a fresh clutch of eggs. If a second clutch of eggs proves to be infertile, it is advisable to try and place some full eggs under the hen to see if she will rear youngsters. Sometimes pairs which have been infertile will manage to produce fertile eggs once they have reared a nest of youngsters. If this fails to do the trick, the birds should be given different partners who have proved their fertility to see if the fault lies with the cock or the hen. Very often the cock is blamed for infertility but this is not always the truth of the matter.

Dead in Shell

Every season a number of fertile eggs will fail to hatch and this can be due to many reasons. Eggs may have become chilled during incubation, the embryo may have died because of some physical disorder or parent birds may have been incorrectly prepared prior to the breeding season.

If an embryo has started to develop inside the egg and the egg becomes chilled for more than a few hours, this will usually prove fatal. It is a wise precaution to check that all sitting hens are on their nests just before dusk. Occasionally cock birds, especially flighted birds, may decide to sit the eggs when the hen leaves the nest to feed. While they may be full of good intentions, cocks will generally fail to sit the eggs throughout the night, and once night has fallen the hen cannot see her way back to the nest. If cock birds have taken over the nest they should be removed from it and the hen allowed to return to her eggs.

Thunder and lightning storms are sometimes said to be the cause of addled eggs, but in fact the only way these storms can affect eggs is if nervous hens are frightened off the nest in the middle of the night, allowing the eggs to become chilled. If birdrooms are situated in a position where it is likely that the birds will be disturbed at night by passing traffic or lights from other houses, a small low-wattage night light can be kept on throughout the hours of darkness to enable disturbed birds to find their way back to the nest. However, most canaries are reliable sitters, not easily disturbed and a night light should be necessary only in extreme cases of night-time disturbance.

The failure of 'full' eggs to hatch may also relate to the humidity level in the birdroom. However, it is a misconception to think that the atmosphere is generally too dry. Eggs are just as likely not to hatch if the humidity is too high as they are if it is too low. Sitting hens will appreciate being allowed to bathe once or twice a week especially during warm weather. This policy can, however, sometimes lead to problems if birds with excessively long feathering are being used. Wet feathers around the legs and flanks can become stuck to the eggs as they dry, resulting in eggs being dragged from the nest the next time the hen leaves to feed.

Black Spot

Sometimes when young canaries hatch they have a small black spot on the right-hand side of the abdomen, under the skin. This is actually caused by a gall bladder malfunction and will often prove to be fatal. Whether the cause is genetic

A Variegated Buff Corona hen, record number 5907. This bird was bred in 1987 and was Second Best Gloster at the 1987 IGBA Club Show, Best Gloster at the North of England Gloster Club Show and the South Coast All Gloster Show, and Best Unflighted Gloster at the Scottish National. The pedigree sheet for this bird appears on p.180.

A Variegated Buff Corona hen, record number 5167. This bird was bred in 1984 from a Yellow Consort cock and a Variegated Buff Corona hen. On the show bench it took the Best in Show award at the East Anglian All Gloster Show, and was a class winner at both the National Exhibition of Cage Birds and the Scottish National. The pedigree sheet for this bird appears on p.176.

A Variegated Buff Consort hen, record number 6395. This bird was bred in 1988 and was Best Consort at the North of England Gloster Club Show and the Scottish National, as an unflighted bird. It was bred from a Heavily Variegated Buff Corona cock mated to a Blue Consort hen.

A Variegated Buff Corona cock, record number 5987, which was bred in 1987. This bird was produced from a Three Parts Dark Buff Corona cock, record number 5215, which appears in this colour section, and a Three Parts Dark Buff Consort hen, record number 5894.

A Heavily Variegated Buff Corona hen, record number 4847, which was bred in 1984. The tilted head on this photograph shows the definite centre of the crest and the regularity of the feathering, radiating from the centre.

A Self Yellow Consort hen, record number 6485, which was bred in 1988. A black and white photograph of this bird appears on p.28. The importance of birds of the yellow-feather type in producing top-quality Gloster Canaries cannot be over-emphasized.

A Cinnamon Buff Consort hen, record number 6368, bred in 1988. This bird has done well in Cinnamon Classes at major shows and its pedigree sheet appears on p.184.

A Three Parts Dark Buff Corona cock, record number 5215, which was bred in 1984. This bird is the father of both the Variegated Buff Corona cock, record number 5987, and the Three Parts Dark Buff Consort cock, record number 5928, which appear in this colour section. On the show bench the Three Parts Dark Corona cock was a class winner as a flighted bird at the National Exhibition of Cage Birds. The pedigree sheet for this bird appears on p.178.

A Three Parts Dark Buff Consort cock, record number 5928, typical of the style of Green Consort essential in maintaining a stud of Gloster Canaries. This bird was bred in 1987 and was also produced from the Three Parts Dark Buff Corona cock, record number 5215. The mother on this occasion was a Cinnamon Buff Consort hen, record number 5705.

A Blue Buff Corona hen, record number 5086. This bird also appears on p.123, pictured showing the opposite profile.

A Blue Buff Consort hen, record number 6176, bred in 1987. The pedigree sheet for this bird appears on p.182. The maternal grandfather of this bird was a brother to the father of the Variegated Buff Corona hen, record number 5907, which appears in this colour section.

or dietary is uncertain, but there is no known cure for the condition.

Occasionally birds born with 'black spot' may survive and live a normal life, but more often, despite being correctly fed, the young will appear to become less active day by day and finally they die. Death is usually caused by the gall bladder rupturing and therefore the 'black spot' disappears when the bird dies.

Poor Feeding

One of the most disappointing aspects of birdkeeping is that some birds will hatch out healthy youngsters and refuse to feed them. This may be because the cock bird is feeding the hen on the nest, so she does not need to leave the nest in order to feed for herself. Removing the cock may force her to leave the nest, and when she returns and sees the gaping youngsters she may begin to feed them. The frequent provision of fresh rearing food and seeded chickweed can help in tempting hens off the nest in order to feed. Babies can be kept alive by feeding them from a small syringe containing a warm mixture of milk, bread and wholewheat cereal biscuits such as Weetabix, made to a sloppy paste-like consistency.

However, it is usually impractical for canary breeders to feed youngsters themselves except on isolated occasions. Sometimes it is possible to transfer the young to another hen who is on clear eggs and is about to finish her incubation period. This bird may prove to be a good feeder and rear the youngsters. When youngsters or eggs are transferred from one nest to another a careful record must be made of these movements. It is pointless rearing canaries if you cannot accurately determine the parentage of the birds produced.

Generally the problem of poor feeding hens diminishes as individual strains of birds become established. Initially the hens maintained by a breeder may come from different sources and prefer different methods of management. As time passes the breeder should build up a stock of his or her own-bred hens which are happy to breed under the specific conditions provided by that fancier. Provided birds are properly fed and managed, at least 90 per cent of hens should breed and rear successfully.

97

Sweating Hens

This term is often used to describe feeding hens which seem to be generally unwell and appear to be wet on the face and breast. This condition is caused by the faecal sac produced by youngsters breaking as the hen tries to clean the nest. The cause of this is often rearing food being either too rich or tainted by poor storage. A change of rearing food may help the situation and the youngsters can be given a clean nest to remove them from harmful bacteria present in the old one.

Ten-Day Itch

Some pairs will successfully rear young until they are about ten days old and then desert them. Where the hen stops brooding her young too soon, removing the perches from the cage may help. This will make the hen perch on the nest pan and encourage her to recommence brooding her chicks. If parent birds refuse to pay any attention to their half-grown youngsters, the only method of saving these babies is to transfer them to other nests containing youngsters of a similar age. Desertion is usually caused by the rearing food used being too rich or being provided in excessive amounts, resulting in parent birds becoming too fit and wanting to go to nest again too quickly.

A nest containing young Gloster Canaries at eight days of age.

Going Light

A number of young canaries suffer a severe and rapid weight loss between being weaned from their parents and becoming able to survive solely on a hard seed diet. This is often referred to as 'going light' and can be minimized by feeding birds correctly once they have been removed from the care of their parents. Niger seed is generally regarded as helpful in preventing young birds going light and should be included in their diet from the time they are separated from their parents until they are fully through the moult. Even so a small percentage of youngsters will always go light no matter what preventive measures are taken.

Removing Cock Birds

There is often a difference of opinion as to whether it is better to allow cock birds to remain with hens while they are sitting and rearing or to remove the cock bird completely from the breeding cage. Some cock birds are nothing but a nuisance in the breeding cage and these should be removed; others are excellent parents and are a great assistance to their mates in rearing youngsters. There is no definite answer to the question; it is largely a matter of personal preference, decided by practical experience of breeding from canaries. Careful observation on the part of the beginner will be a great help in deciding whether or not to remove the cock.

Breeding from canaries may seem to be a complicated business, but it becomes easier with experience. If a good diet and sound management routine which suit both the breeder and the birds have been formulated, breeding should be fairly straightforward. Remember that even very experienced breeders can have poor breeding seasons: this is a fact of life when breeding from any form of livestock.

11 Moulting

The moult is a particularly stressful time for canaries and it is important that everything is done to ensure this will be as trouble-free as possible. As the breeding season progresses, birds which have been rearing youngsters will begin to lose their 'edge' and, by the middle of summer, most will be ready to start moulting. With the moult taking place between the breeding season and the show season, some breeders may think this is a quiet time of year, but it is very important that routine general management tasks are not overlooked.

Additional General Management
In addition to the usual routine tasks, all the equipment used during the breeding season will need to be cleaned and stored in readiness for the following year. Used nest pans must have their old felts and any loose dirt removed and discarded as they become vacant, before being soaked in a solution of bleach, rinsed clean and dried prior to storing. Feeding pots used specifically during the breeding season also need to be thoroughly cleaned before being stored away until they are needed again. Once breeding cages become vacant they must be thoroughly cleaned and disinfected before being used as stock cages.

This is also the time of the year to perform any general maintenance which may be required on the fabric of the birdroom. Roofs should be checked to make sure they are sound and the exteriors of timber birdrooms will benefit from being treated with wood preservative. It is wise to make good any repairs which may be necessary during the summer months when the evenings are lighter and the weather generally better. For the exhibitor there will be precious little time available later in the year to perform these essential tasks.

Housing
As adults finish breeding, hens should be moved into flight cages measuring at least 4 ft (1.2 m) in length, usually double or treble breeders with the slides removed. They should be kept in groups of six or seven, and you should be careful to separate Consorts from Coronas. Adult cock birds are generally better housed individually, in smaller cages measuring about 16 in (40 cm) in length. Where possible, adult birds should not be moved to other cages until they have successfully completed their moult. Canaries which are experiencing a full moult, with their complete plumage, including tail and flight feathers, being replaced, appreciate a calm, restful atmosphere. Undue disturbances tend to cause additional stress, which will be detrimental to their general condition and health.

Young Coronas can be housed initially in twos or threes, in cages about half the size used for adult hens. As young Coronas develop, those which show exhibition potential can be removed and housed on their own in readiness for show training. If there is excessive fighting, squabbling and feather plucking among groups of young Coronas, offenders should be removed. In many cases a short period in the company of a cage of adult hens should soon improve the conduct of younger birds. However, excessive fighting between young Coronas is rarely a problem, provided they are housed separately from Consorts. Young Consorts may be kept in larger groups, either in aviaries or flight cages, until they have virtually completed the moult. A little fighting and feather-plucking among Consorts is not as potentially damaging to their exhibition potential as it can be with Coronas.

Feeding
At this time adult birds should be fed a basic diet of plain canary seed, grit and clean water. Additionally, twice a week they can receive a little condition seed, rearing food with added SA37 and a liquid vitamin supplement such as Collavet in their drinking water. These 'extras' should not be provided all at the same time, but on separate days, and you should be careful not to overfeed adult cock birds. Adult cocks seem particularly prone to digestive disorders during

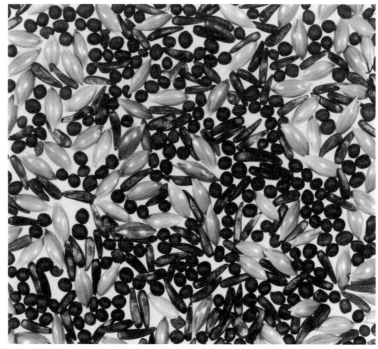

A seed mixture, consisting of plain canary seed, rubsen rape and niger seed, suitable for young Gloster Canaries during the summer months.

the moult and a diet which is too rich often results in birds having dirty vents. Any birds with soiled vents should be caught up and the dirt soaked in warm water until it is loosened and can be removed without causing the bird any physical discomfort.

The majority of unflighted birds will usually have progressed on to a seed diet containing about 50 per cent plain canary seed, 35 per cent rape seed and 15 per cent niger seed by the time adult birds begin their moult. This can be provided in open pots but must be sieved daily, to remove dust and dirt, before being replenished with fresh seed. The seed mixture should have a greater proportion of canary seed added gradually until, by the beginning of autumn, unflighted birds have progressed on to a basic seed diet consisting purely of plain canary seed. Young birds will require a daily supply of rearing food throughout the summer months and also appreciate small amounts of crushed hemp on a daily basis. Both adults and youngsters will benefit from the provision of any suitable source of wild seeds, such as greater plantain, sea arrow grass, redshank, meadow sweet and seeding grass.

Maximization of Feather Quality Potential

In addition to proper housing and feeding, canaries require ample opportunity to bathe during the moult. It is impossible to provide your birds with too many baths at this time. Spraying with warm water will also be beneficial and helps to promote the best possible feather quality in your stock. Particular attention should be paid to the crests of Coronas when spraying, ensuring the direction of the spray encourages the plumage to radiate from the centre of the crest, equally in all directions. During the summer months, birds can be sprayed quite heavily, allowing the maximum penetration of water. Because of the provision of ample baths and regular spraying, it is particularly important for the birdroom to be adequately ventilated: a stuffy, musty, damp atmosphere is to be avoided at all costs in any birdroom. It is also advisable to dust all birds with mite powder during the summer months. This not only helps to deter red mite and northern mite, but also prevents any infestation by feather mite or depluming mite. If birds have their new plumage attacked by mite at a very early stage of development this will spoil their appearance for the rest of the year.

A good moult is invaluable for the exhibitor. When birds come through the moult quickly and cleanly, this permits a much wider choice of potential exhibits throughout the show season. Exhibiting birds which have not quite completed their moult at early shows is a very risky business and can ruin them for the remainder of the show season. Any laziness or lack of attention to detail on the part of the birdkeeper during the summer months can result not only in a disappointing show season, but also in a poor breeding season for the following year.

12 Ailments

The majority of Gloster Canaries will remain fit, healthy and free from ailments and diseases throughout their life. The most important factors in keeping birds fit and healthy are the provision of good accommodation, a variety of good-quality foodstuffs and sound general management practices. Birds kept in damp, draughty birdrooms in dirty cages or fed on a poor-quality diet, supplied in dirty seed hoppers and drinkers, will rarely be fully fit. Any of these undesirable conditions can be instrumental in allowing individual studs of birds to suffer regularly from a whole range of ailments and diseases, which at the very least cause severe discomfort to the birds, and more often result in premature death. Birds kept in a stressful environment have a greatly reduced natural

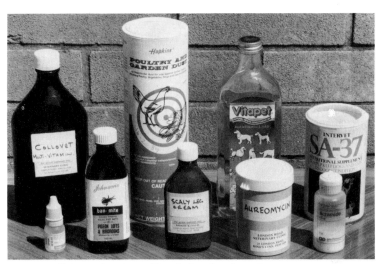

Various medicines and tonics useful to the breeder of canaries.

resistance to disease and therefore badly maintained birds are far more prone to illness. To overlook the basics of good husbandry when maintaining any form of livestock is simply asking for trouble, and medicines and 'magic potions' can do nothing in the long term to combat persistent laxity on the part of the birdkeeper.

However, even in the cleanest and best-organized bird-rooms, problems with the health of stock can arise from time to time. These health problems fall into two main categories, those for which a cure can be effected by the use of basic nursing practices and simple medicines, and those which require the use of more complex and powerful medicines such as antibiotics, which are only available on prescription. Even when antibiotics are employed in the treatment of small birds, some complaints will be incurable, often because insufficient qualified research has been done with regard to these species.

Hospital Cage

Because small birds have a high metabolic rate, diseases which cause loss of appetite or failure to assimilate food correctly, resulting in weight loss or fluid loss, lead rapidly to dehydration and an energy imbalance. In order to minimize these effects it is important to keep sick birds in a warm, stress-free environment. This is most easily achieved by using a hospital cage, the temperature of which is controlled by means of a thermostat. This allows individual sick birds to be kept in the best possible environment, without affecting the conditions of other birds within the same birdroom. In order to give sick birds the best chance of being cured, it is usually necessary to raise the temperature inside the hospital cage to about 80°F (27°C) and provide the prescribed medicine in addition to seed, rearing food, grit and water (if it has not been replaced by the prescribed medicine). Canaries are, however, very susceptible to changes in temperature and therefore it is wise to increase gradually to the required level the temperature of the hospital cage containing a sick bird, rather than place the bird directly into a hospital cage which has already been warmed up. It is essential that once the treatment has effected a cure, the temperature of the cage is gradually reduced over a period of days until it is down to birdroom temperature, giving the treated bird every opportunity to adjust.

While it may be necessary to use a hospital cage only on very rare occasions, it is usually a good investment for the birdkeeper who has a stud of quality birds. Individual birds within good studs are often impossible to replace and therefore must be given the best possible chance of recovering from illness.

Egg Binding

This condition obviously affects only hens and the term means being temporarily unable to pass an egg normally. In reality it should be a very rare problem within a stud of canaries provided birds have been given a well-balanced diet containing adequate amounts of calcium and vitamin D. Vitamin D is essential for the absorption of calcium by birds and obviously when hens are laying they need additional reserves of calcium to produce their eggshells. Vitamin D is obtained naturally from sunlight, but because birds are normally housed indoors, some form of additional vitamin D should be provided. Cod liver oil is a good natural source and vitamin D is also present in many commercially available vitamin preparations. The calcium required should be present in the regular grit supplies given to birds, particularly in limestone grit and oystershell grit. In severe cases of calcium deficiency, calcium syrup or calcium injections can be used to rectify the problem, provided the birds are not deficient in vitamin D.

The symptoms of egg binding are that the hen looks most unwell, her feathers are ruffled in an attempt to create maximum warmth and generally she will sit huddled up in a cage corner. On closer examination some swelling of the abdomen will usually be detected.

Treatment is to place the bird in a hospital cage and gradually raise the temperature to 80°F (27°C). In addition to the normal diet, some extra form of vitamin D and calcium should be made available. The offending egg is usually laid without too much difficulty and the bird can then be re-acclimatized to normal birdroom temperatures. It is generally unnecessary to resort to any external treatment of the vent in order to cure this problem.

Colds and Chills

These are generally caused by keeping birds in unsuitable conditions which are either too damp or too draughty, or both. Symptoms are similar to those seen in egg-bound hens, but without the abdominal swelling. Placing affected birds in a hospital cage, as previously described, will usually help them to recover from these complaints. A hospital cage cannot, however, do anything to remove the original cause of the problem: this can be achieved only by the birdkeeper deciding to house his or her stock in suitable conditions.

Going Light

This term is used by birdkeepers to describe a condition whereby birds suffer a severe and rapid weight loss which is particularly noticeable on the breast, allowing the breast bone to be felt prominently beneath the skin. The condition is often accompanied by symptoms similar to those associated with colds and chills, and loose droppings or diarrhoea. A temporary cure can often be obtained by placing the bird in a warm hospital cage, but as soon as it is returned to a normal environment the original symptoms reappear. An exact cause of the condition has not been determined, probably because it can be due to a variety of factors. The only way to effect a long-term cure is to seek professional advice from a veterinary surgeon. In all probability it will be necessary to take various samples in order to produce cultures which can then be examined for the presence of harmful organisms. The medicine prescribed will depend on the findings made by this examination.

Respiratory Disorders

Birds are particularly susceptible to respiratory disorders, some of which are very difficult to cure. The cause of these disorders can be parasitic, bacterial, fungal, viral or environmental. The two most common parasites to affect the respiratory tract are airsac mite and gape worms. Mite may be controlled by the use of a dichlorvos strip (see **Mite** p.108) in the birdroom. Gape worm can usually be treated successfully with wormers such as benzimidazole or levamisole. Environmental causes can include irritant gases from car exhausts, burning fat or some types of paint and are simply remedied by removing the cause of the problem from the proximity of your birds. Bacterial infections such as mycoplasmas, viral infections such as Newcastle's disease, and fungal infections, responsible for aspergillosis, all require veterinary assistance to have any hope of limiting outbreaks. While aspergillosis is particularly difficult to cure, it is often caused by feeding mouldy food, highlighting the importance of feeding only clean, good-quality, fresh food.

Worms
Parasitic worms of the digestive system, such as roundworms and threadworms, may be picked up by canaries, but usually only if birds are kept in outside flights and aviaries which allow contact with wild birds. Good hygiene in the birdroom and the quarantine of birds acquired from other sources will help to prevent the transmission of worms from one bird to another. Typical symptoms include diarrhoea, weight loss and lifelessness. Effective treatment can be achieved by using piperazine or levamisole worming preparations, coupled with improved hygiene.

Crop Disorders
The most common of these is sour crop, which results in involuntary regurgitation of food and/or diarrhoea. It may be due to bacteria or yeasts and the effective treatment depends on the use of antibiotics or antifungal agents according to the specific cause. In either case it will be necessary to consult your veterinary surgeon.

Mite
There are various different forms of mite which can infest canaries, and birdkeepers must be ever watchful for the first signs of outbreaks of these pests within the birdroom. Good general management and regular treatment of cages and nest felts, prior to the breeding season, with preparations such as Ban Mite will help to keep the birdroom free from these pests. Birds also need to be properly treated with mite powder twice a year as a matter of routine, usually before and after the breeding season. Should outbreaks occur, specific treatment of individual birds can be undertaken using mite

powder, and cages can be treated with aerosol sprays. Additionally an anti-insect strip containing dichlorvos can be introduced to the birdroom and this will help to exterminate these pests. Great care must be taken in selecting a suitable strip as some are harmful to birds. Vapona strips are quite widely used and, provided they are installed exactly to the manufacturer's recommendations, should not prove lethal to birds. However, there could be some reservations about using them continually in order to prevent outbreaks of mite as they may make some birds drowsy and lethargic. When using any treatment, take care to ensure food supplies do not become contaminated.

Northern Mite

In the terminology of canary breeders 'northern mite' refers to an extremely virulent and troublesome form of mite which seems to infest birdrooms just as it pleases. In theory, northern mite should spend the whole of its life on the host, and be passed from bird to bird only by physical contact. The pest which is so troublesome to canary breeders does not follow this behaviour. The first sign of the pest is usually when they are seen as small dark dots swarming in specific cages. Birds generally seem irritated and, if left unchecked, these mite will overrun the largest birdroom in a very short space of time. Maintaining clean, regularly painted cages is a great asset in being able to spot infestation while it is still limited to one or two cages. Remedial action must be taken at the first sign of any outbreak of this mite.

Red Mite

At one time these were extremely prevalent in studs of canaries, but modern treatments have largely eradicated them. Red mite are said to attack birds only at night, spending the daylight hours hidden in cracks and crevices in cages and aviaries. It should be remembered, however, that red mite appear to be red only when they are engorged with blood and if spotted early enough they may be black or grey in appearance. Any outbreaks should be combated by treating both the cages and the birds with appropriate preparations.

Airsac Mite

This parasite affects the membranes of the respiratory system, resulting in a loss of voice and song and giving rise to breathing difficulties. It is best treated by means of preparations designed to create an atmosphere which is lethal to mite.

Scaly Face or Scaly Leg

This complaint is caused by a mite, cnemidocoptes, which burrows into the outer layers of the skin, creating a honeycombed effect on the beak or legs. It may occasionally occur in canaries, although it is more common in other species, and can be treated with Scaly Face Cream or benzyl benzoate. Liquid paraffin may help to restore the appearance of the legs.

Feather Mite

There are various forms of feather mite or depluming mite which can affect all birds. First signs of infestation can be seen in the larger wing and tail feathers, which will appear to be worn away near to the central spine of the feather. If left unchecked these mites will infest the central spines of newly developing feathers, preventing them from forming properly. Correct treatment with mite powder is usually quite effective but obviously plumage will remain damaged until moulted out.

Lice

Birds can also be infested with lice, which spend the whole of their life cycle on the bird and in extreme cases can cause feather plucking. Treatment to eradicate lice is similar to that used to combat mite.

Feather Cysts

Feather cysts, often called 'lumps', can become quite common in some breeds of canary, especially if there is a tendency to breed for a very soft, curled or tufted type of feather. Cysts are generally found on the wings, but may occur in other areas, and are caused by the feather being too soft to break through the skin and develop normally. The feather continues to grow inside the skin and is accompanied by an oily discharge produced by glands. Sometimes the feather cyst may become infected, which leads to more serious complications. The treatment involves careful incision of the cyst, removal of the discharge and general cleaning of the wound, and should not be undertaken by anyone unqualified to do so. This is not a cure, however, as birds which have a problem with feather cysts will usually produce more with each successive moult. The cure is to prevent birds with this type of feather being bred by careful examination of the feather quality of all stock used for breeding purposes.

Soft Moult
This is a term generally used to describe a condition whereby birds moult out of season or become stuck in the moult. The cause is often stress, which can be due to a variety of factors, including sudden temperature changes or irregular lighting conditions. Affected birds should be placed in a stress-free environment and not subjected to extremes of temperature or excessive lighting.

Eye Infections
Birds quite commonly suffer from irritations and infections of the eyes. The causes can range from draughty quarters or the use of too fine a sawdust as cage floor coverings, to not cleaning perches properly on a regular basis or fighting. Minor eye irritations can be eased by gently bathing the affected eye with a solution of boracic acid, mixed to the manufacturer's instructions: this is readily available at most chemists. Bathing should be done once a day and should there be no improvement, veterinary assistance will be required. Serious eye infections or persistent irritations may be successfully treated with preparations such as chloramphenicol, which is available only on prescription.

Slip Claw
This means that the back claw is displaced, often turned under the ball of the foot, but sometimes dislodged so that it stands off the perch. This fault is often associated with birds which have been sole nestlings and have not had the support of other youngsters in the nest. If the claw is turned under the foot in young birds, it can be carefully strapped back to its normal position for a couple of weeks and will often right itself.

Sore Feet and Legs

There are various causes of birds suffering from sore feet and legs, including cnemidocoptes, the mite responsible for scaly face and scaly leg; bacterial infection causing a swelling of the pad of the foot, generally called bumblefoot; high-protein diets causing gout; providing perches of an unsuitable diameter; and keeping birds in unclean conditions. Scaly leg can be treated as previously described. Bumblefoot will need treating with antibiotics and may also require surgical drainage of the infected foot. Gout tends to produce a swelling of joints, often with a yellowish discoloration visible through the skin. This complaint can usually be treated by reducing protein levels in the diet and increasing the supply of vitamin A, although surgical lancing may be required in some cases. Where swelling of the legs occurs, birds wearing an identification ring on their leg may need to have this removed, to prevent the supply of blood to the foot being restricted. Birds' feet and legs should be kept clean at all times. Birds with dirty feet should be caught and their feet gently bathed until clean. Attention should also be paid to toe-nails, which if they become excessively long will need to be trimmed, taking care not to cut into the central vein of the nail. Should this vein be cut, bleeding will occur and this should be treated with antiseptic and stemmed by the application of silver nitrate or a styptic pencil.

Broken Legs and Wings

In the unfortunate event of a bird suffering from a broken leg or wing, it may be possible to repair the damage by using basic first aid. Broken legs can sometimes be splinted using insulation tape, allowing a period of at least three weeks for the damage to heal. Broken wings can be strapped, again allowing at least three weeks before removing the strapping, but this is less likely to be successful.

Fits and Strokes

Occasionally birds will suffer from fits or strokes. In both cases affected birds should be placed on their own in a stress-free environment and allowed to recover naturally. Birds suffering from a fit will usually make a full recovery in the short term but will continue to be susceptible to this complaint. Remember that this may be a genetic disorder and breeding from birds which are prone to fits will inevitably result in large numbers of birds which suffer from fits being produced. Birds which have had a stroke will rarely make an adequate recovery and often the only course of action is to have them humanely destroyed.

Common Sense
Outbreaks of the diseases which are generally associated with small birds such as canaries can usually be minimized by good general management and the adoption of sensible quarantine procedures when introducing newly acquired stock. While many ailments can be treated using simple basic medicines, certain complaints can be cured only with the assistance of professional advice. Medicines supplied on prescription, such as antibiotics, are to combat specific diseases in specific individuals. They should not be used in a misguided attempt to prevent diseases occurring. This is not their function and such a policy will serve only to make these medicines less effective in combating outbreaks of specific diseases. The best method of limiting and controlling diseases in the birdroom is the combination of good feeding, good hygiene and keen observation. Naturally these take time and effort on the part of the birdkeeper, but there is no practical substitute for the essentials of good husbandry.

13   Colour Variations

There are a number of colour mutations which are catered for within the Gloster Canary Fancy. These are traditional mutations which have been known in the canary world for many years. Other colour mutations which appear in Gloster Canaries are not recognized and any Gloster which displays any of these colours immediately becomes re-classified as a New Colour Canary.

In order to make sense of the mutations present and understand their genetic characteristics, it is necessary to realize that the 'Normal' form of the canary, to which all other mutations relate, is a Self Green canary: that is to say, a green canary which shows no variegated markings whatsoever, not even one light feather or light foot or variegated mark on the beak. Such birds are very rarely seen, but it is to these that other mutations relate. The reason very few Self Greens are seen is because of the widespread use of Variegated birds, which to many people are far more visually attractive than the original Self Green. This means that nearly every domesticated canary is some form of the Variegated mutation, and this mutation produces areas of clear plumage, generally yellow in colour.

Variegated

The Variegated mutation has become so well established in canaries that it is virtually impossible to eradicate. Genetically any bird which shows one or more light feather or a light mark on its feet, legs or beak, must be regarded as being Variegated. Because they are so widespread, Variegated birds have been split into different groups according to the degree of variegation shown. In the Gloster Fancy, classes are

An Unflighted Variegated Buff Corona cock which was a class winner at both the National Exhibition of Cage Birds and the Scottish National. The record number of this bird is 4782 and it was bred in 1983. A sister of this bird was the mother of the Corona hen, record number 5167, featured on p.176.

provided for Variegated Green Buffs, known simply as Buffs, and for Three Parts Dark to Self Green Buffs, generally referred to as Three Parts Darks. Genetically there is no difference between these two types, but it makes sense to split Variegateds into two classes, in view of the number being bred and exhibited. The decision as to where the border should be drawn between Light Variegateds and Dark Variegateds is simply a matter of choosing a dividing line which will produce two classes of approximately equal numbers.

In genetic terms the Variegated mutation is recessive and this accounts for the fact that virtually no pure-bred Self Green canaries exist today. When a visual Variegated bird is mated to a genetically pure Self, all the young produced will in theory be visual Selfs, but all will carry the gene responsible for Variegated in their genetic make-up. When two of these visual Selfs which carry the gene for Variegated in their make-up are mated together, one quarter of the young produced will be visual Variegateds, one quarter will be visual Selfs which are genetically pure, and the remainder will be visual Selfs which carry the Variegated gene. If a visual Variegated is mated to a visual Self which carries the Variegated gene, half the youngsters should be visual Variegateds and half will be visual Selfs carrying the Variegated gene in their make-up. Mating two Variegated birds together should result in all the young produced being visual Variegateds.

It can be seen that, in quite a short space of time, the use of Variegated birds will result in a virtual absence of genetically pure Selfs. This stage had already been reached by the time the Gloster Canary was 'born'. Therefore birds which display some visual form of variegation are now the 'Normal' and birds showing no light markings whatsoever are a rarity. Because the Variegated mutation is present in virtually all Gloster Canaries, the term 'Normal' as used to describe matings involving other mutations, such as Cinnamon and White, actually refers to a Green Variegated bird. For the purposes of explaining the genetic characteristics of other mutations it is irrelevant whether these 'Normal' birds are Lightly Variegated, Variegated, Heavily Variegated, Three Parts Dark or Foul Marked. It is quite superfluous to employ a full written description, provided the reader is aware of this situation.

Lightly Variegated birds tend to have far more popular appeal than Heavily Variegated, Three Parts Dark and Foul Marked specimens. Breeders should not, however, try to build up a stud of Gloster Canaries which contains nothing but Lightly Variegated birds. The use of Dark birds, especially Dark birds of the yellow-feather type, is imperative in order to maintain good quality and type in a stud of Gloster Canaries. A stud should contain an absolute maximum of 25 per cent Lightly Variegated birds, and will probably progress much more rapidly if an even smaller percentage of Light birds is maintained.

Cinnamon

The Cinnamon mutation in canaries is one of the oldest established colour variations associated with the species. Virtually all other breeds of type standard canaries make provision for Cinnamon birds, and the Gloster Canary Fancy is no exception to this general rule.

The mutation has the effect of reducing the intensity of the black pigments which would normally be present in the plumage of canaries. When this occurs, non-variegated plumage should ideally become a very similar colour to that of freshly ground cinnamon. The Cinnamon mutation does not, however, alter the ground colour of the bird, which remains yellow. Therefore if a Clear Cinnamon, one which shows no non-variegated plumage, is produced, it will on first inspection appear to be very similar to a Clear Normal bird. However the Cinnamon mutation does also affect the eye colour of birds, reducing the eye pigments from black to a reddish colour. This redness can be seen quite clearly in certain lighting conditions, usually when the bird is viewed in direct specular lighting.

Genetically the mutation is sex-linked, and this means that the colour of youngsters produced from Normal × Cinnamon pairings depends on the colour and sex of the parents. The results obtained by mating a Cinnamon cock to a Normal hen are different from those produced by pairing a Normal cock to a Cinnamon hen. The sex-linked nature of the mutation also makes it impossible for hens to carry the Cinnamon mutation in hidden form: if a hen inherits the gene responsible for the Cinnamon mutation from her parents, she will be a Cinnamon. However, cocks can be of Normal appearance, and carry the Cinnamon mutation hidden within their genetic make-up. In the canary fancy, these birds are generally referred to as Cinnamon carrier cocks but in mating lists they would usually be described as 'Normal/Cinnamon cocks'.

In order to produce visual Cinnamons, the first stage is to obtain either a Cinnamon cock or a Normal cock which is a Cinnamon carrier. When either of these birds is mated to a Normal hen, some visual Cinnamon hens should be produced. In the case of a visual Cinnamon cock, all the hens will be Cinnamons, and if a Cinnamon carrier cock is used, then half the hens bred should be visual Cinnamons. All the cocks produced from a Cinnamon cock mated to a Normal hen will be visual Normals, and all will be Cinnamon carriers. Only half the cocks produced from matings between a Cinnamon carrier cock and a Normal hen will be Cinnamon carriers, the remainder being pure Normals. As there is no sure method of differentiating between pure Normal cocks and Cinnamon carrier cocks, simply by visual inspection, cock birds produced from matings between Cinnamon carrier cocks and Normal hens cannot be guaranteed as Cinnamon carriers, unless they have previously been test mated.

A certain method of breeding Cinnamon carrier cocks is to mate a Normal cock to a Cinnamon hen: all the hens produced will be Normals and all the cocks will be Cinnamon carriers. Indeed, breeders will probably find that there is a shortage of visual Cinnamon cock Gloster Canaries and therefore it is necessary to use either a visual Cinnamon hen or a Cinnamon carrier cock in order to establish a stock of Cinnamons. In order to produce visual Cinnamon cocks it is necessary for both parent birds to have the gene responsible for the Cinnamon mutation in their genetic make-up. Usually, if breeders wish to produce visual Cinnamon cocks, a Cinnamon carrier cock will be mated to a visual Cinnamon hen. From such a mating half the cocks produced should be visual Cinnamons, the remainder all being Cinnamon carriers.

A Cinnamon Consort hen of remarkable type and quality which has been successfully exhibited on several occasions.

Half the hens produced should also be visual Cinnamons, the remainder being pure Normal hens. Cinnamon cocks are particularly useful in the production of Fawns, which are white ground Cinnamons, and the methods of producing these birds will be described in detail in the section dealing with White and Allied to White Glosters. The mating together of a visual Cinnamon cock and a visual Cinnamon hen will produce just Cinnamon youngsters, but such matings tend to be only of academic interest to the breeder of exhibition quality Gloster Canaries.

While other sections of the canary fancy may stick rigidly to Cinnamon × Cinnamon matings, this is not the case in the Gloster Canary Fancy. The most usual pairings utilized to produce Cinnamon Glosters are Normal cock × Cinnamon hen and Cinnamon carrier cock × Normal hen. Mating a Normal cock to a Cinnamon hen produces Cinnamon carrier cocks, which can then be mated to Normal hens to breed a percentage of visual Cinnamon hens. Naturally, using just these two matings makes it impossible to produce visual Cinnamon cocks, but this is of little consequence to the exhibitor, as Cinnamon cocks and Cinnamon hens are both exhibited in the same class. The preference for Cinnamon hens is due to the fact that hens tend to display better type and size than cocks, and therefore generally have an advantage on the show bench.

The use of Normal × Cinnamon matings does not in practice seem to be in any way detrimental to the colour of the Cinnamons produced. The fact that there are some very pale, sandy-coloured Cinnamons to be seen in the Gloster Fancy should not be attributed to the use of Normal × Cinnamon matings. This poor colour is more probably due to the use of badly coloured Cinnamons initially. Obviously if these poor-coloured birds are used to establish Cinnamons in your stud, this will be reflected in the colour of any Cinnamons produced.

The Cinnamon mutation, in addition to displaying a change of colour, also seems to affect the structure of the feather. Cinnamons generally have a finer, softer feather than Normals. In practical terms this means that the apparent visual type of Cinnamons is generally poorer than that of Normals. Because the feather has less 'bulk', Cinnamons can appear to lack a little substance. For this reason it is most unusual to mate Cinnamons to yellow-feathered birds, as this tends to produce an even finer feather and therefore an even greater decline in the apparent type displayed. The breeder who maintains only a small stud of birds generally cannot afford to risk producing yellow-feathered Cinnamons because of their limitations as exhibition birds. However, if a larger stud is being maintained it may be acceptable to make pairings where there is the chance that some yellow-feathered Cinnamons will be produced. Such matings would not be made with a view to breeding yellow-feathered Cinnamons, but for other reasons associated with the visual characteristics and relationship between the specific individual birds used in the mating.

Because the Cinnamon mutation is associated with a finer feather texture, some breeders believe it is instrumental in producing birds of good feather quality. This is not necessarily true: while some Cinnamons have very good feather quality and, when properly mated, can reasonably be expected to produce youngsters which show good feather quality, there are plenty of coarse rough-feathered Cinnamons about, which can have only an adverse effect on the feather quality of any youngsters they produce. Equally Cinnamons of good feather quality cannot be expected to work miracles with regard to improving feather quality in birds which lack this feature. More often than not, if birds of poor feather quality are mated to Cinnamons, this will ruin the feather quality of all the youngsters produced, regardless of colour.

Cinnamons are no more delicate or less productive than any other colour of canary and can help to add variety of colour and interest to any stud of Glosters. The only area where caution needs to be exercised is in the retention of Normal cock birds bred from Normal/Cinnamon cocks mated to Normal hens. As it is impossible to determine whether or not such cocks are Cinnamon carriers before breeding from them, the excessive use of these birds could lead to a small stud being overrun with Cinnamons. When selecting Cinnamons to be used as stock birds in a stud of exhibition Gloster Canaries, they should be assessed as Gloster Canaries, and the essential features of the breed must not be ignored just for the sake of maintaining some Cinnamon coloured birds.

A list of mating expectations from Cinnamons is included on p.170 for easy reference.

White and Allied to White

The White mutation as it applies to Gloster Canaries is the traditional Dominant White mutation, which has the effect of reducing the ground colour of the bird from yellow to white. Therefore any variegated areas of plumage appear white, while non-variegated plumage has a bluish cast. White Glosters are often called Blues except when they are very Lightly Variegated specimens. For simplicity Self Blues, Variegated Blues and Clear Whites will all be referred to as Whites in this chapter. The Recessive White mutation, which in theory could be produced in a Gloster Canary, is not relevant to the Gloster Fancy and should be categorized as a New Colour Canary.

The Dominant White mutation is, as the name suggests, genetically dominant. As is often the case with genetically dominant mutations, a double factor of this mutation is generally regarded as being lethal. It is therefore inadvisable to mate two Whites together. Double factor birds usually die when very young and death may even occur prior to hatching, during the very early stages of embryo development. Visual Dominant White canaries carry only one gene for the White mutation, this being matched to a Normal gene, and in genetic terms should be regarded as single factor Whites or White (s.f.). Only Whites that carry two genes for the White mutation would be termed double factors or White (d.f.). Because of the lethal gene combination, these birds can be regarded as being of purely academic interest. The White mutation is not in any way sex-linked, and it is therefore irrelevant whether a White cock or White hen is used in matings to Normal birds, as far as the percentages and sex of White birds produced are concerned. Pairings made between a Normal and a visual White will in theory produce 50 per cent Normal and 50 per cent White youngsters. These can be either cocks or hens and can be anything from Self Blues through to Clear Whites, depending on the variegation inherited from their parents. If two Whites were mated together, in theory half the young produced would be Whites, all of which would be single factor birds, one quarter of the young would be Normals and the remaining quarter would all be double factor Whites. However, the double factor, being a lethal combination, would mean that these birds should not survive to maturity. If it was possible to produce a double factor White, and breed from it by mating it to a Normal, theoretically all the young produced would be single factor Whites. Any white ground bird which produces a yellow ground bird must be a single factor White.

Despite the lethal nature of a double dose of the gene responsible for producing white ground birds, single factor Whites should be no less robust or fertile than Glosters of other colours. The presence of white ground birds in a stud of Glosters can help to add visual variety to the collection. If you wish to breed examples of White or Allied to White Canaries, it is essential to breed from a visual white ground bird. The gene for the White mutation cannot be inherited from a yellow ground bird, and therefore white ground birds cannot be bred by mating two yellow ground birds together.

A Blue Corona hen which was Best Gloster Canary at the 1983 Scottish National and Best White Gloster on many occasions. This bird was bred in 1983 and its record number is 5086.

Before deciding to maintain some Whites, it is advisable to build up a good foundation stock of Normal buffs and yellows. Whites are a popular colour in the Gloster Fancy and good examples tend to do well on the show bench, often winning section specials. Indeed, white ground Gloster Canaries have taken major honours at both the IGBA Club Show and the National Exhibition of Cage Birds which, for Gloster Canary breeders in the UK, are probably the two most prestigious events in the exhibition calender.

Generally it is easier to concentrate on Heavily Variegated to Self birds when establishing Whites. Although good-quality Clear Whites can be produced, they often tend to lack substance. The vast majority of White Glosters produced are buff-feathered birds and should always be regarded as being of the buff-feather type, unless you have definite information to the contrary. Usually white ground birds are mated to yellow ground birds of the buff-feather type, and often these will be birds which are Heavily Variegated or darker. For these pairings it is important to try and use yellow ground birds which have some birds of the yellow-feather type in their pedigree, in order to maintain good feather quality in the birds produced.

Occasionally, Normal birds which have not seen a White before can be quite startled by these birds; exhibitors might be well advised to keep an odd White in the birdroom so that other stock becomes accustomed to seeing Whites. It would be a great pity if you had a bird in contention for a major award which 'went to pieces' at a critical moment because it happened to see a White canary for the first time. Judging the White classes can be most interesting, as it is necessary to assess the relative merits of flighted and unflighted birds, cocks and hens, Blues, Fawns and Clears, all in the same class. With Blues, preference should be given to birds of a slate blue colour rather than to those which have a brownish cast. However, because cocks tend to display better colour than hens, and hens tend to show better type than cocks, getting the balance right can be quite a challenge to the judge.

Fawn is the term used in the canary fancy to describe white ground Cinnamons and in order to produce birds of this colour it is necessary to combine the White and Cinnamon mutations. The first step towards producing Fawns is to mate a visual Cinnamon cock to a White hen. In theory one quarter of the young produced will be Fawn hens, and a further quarter will be White Cinnamon carrier cocks, which can also be utilized in breeding Fawns. The remaining youngsters should either be Normal Cinnamon carrier cocks or visual Cinnamon hens, and will be no more useful in producing Fawns than birds of a similar genetic make-up, bred from pairings which do not include a White parent bird.

Should a Cinnamon cock not be available, then progress will have to be made by mating a Normal Cinnamon carrier cock to a White hen. In theory one eighth of the young produced should be Fawn hens. If this mating is not possible, a White cock should be paired to a Cinnamon hen; one quarter of the young produced should be White cocks and all will be Cinnamon carriers. However, the White hens produced from this mating cannot carry the Cinnamon gene and therefore are no more likely to produce Fawns than any other White hen. If a White Cinnamon carrier cock is then mated to a Normal hen, one eighth of the young produced should be Fawn hens, and if a White Cinnamon carrier cock is mated to a Cinnamon hen, one quarter of the youngsters produced will in theory be Fawns, and these can be either cocks or hens. When a Normal Cinnamon carrier cock is mated to a Fawn hen this should produce one quarter Fawn youngsters, which may be either cocks or hens. Mating a Cinnamon cock to a Fawn hen will produce half Fawn youngsters and once again these may be either cocks or hens. If a Fawn cock is mated to a Normal hen, then one quarter of the young should be Fawns, but all will be hens. Whites and Fawns should not be mated together, as this will involve the lethal double factor which occurs when two genes for the White mutation are matched together in the same bird.

The theoretical percentages of each colour produced from these matings can vary considerably in practice, and breeders may well find that when matings are employed where only one eighth of the young produced will have the desired genetic make-up, progress can be very slow indeed. It always seems to be the case that when a specific colour is required, everything but that colour will be produced. The production of Fawn canaries is much easier if it is possible to use a visual Cinnamon cock initially. Where a visual Cinnamon cock is not available it can take two or three seasons to produce anything which will be useful with regard to producing Fawns.

Because Fawns are exhibited in the White and Allied to White classes, and have to compete against Blues, they are not usually particularly successful on the show bench. The combination of the Cinnamon mutation and the White mutation has a tendency to produce birds which appear to lack substance, when compared to Whites produced from Normal × White pairings. For the breeder who maintains only a small exhibition stud, breeding Fawns can therefore be rather counter-productive as far as success on the show bench is concerned. However, the breeder who has a larger stud at his or her disposal may find that producing good-quality Fawns is an interesting challenge, and there tends to be a good demand within the fancy generally for these birds.

Once again, when selecting Whites or Fawns to be used in a stud of exhibition Gloster Canaries, birds must be assessed as Gloster Canaries and not retained just because they happen to be of a particular colour. Just as the genes responsible for the different colour mutations can be passed from generation to generation, so can the genes which are responsible for poor type, feather faults and other undesirable features be passed on to the young produced.

A list of mating expectations from Whites is included on p.171 for easy reference.

Grizzle

The Grizzle Corona is a bird which displays a clear or grizzled crest, as opposed to the dark crest seen in the vast majority of Gloster Canaries. This particular type of marking probably has its origins in the old Lancashire Coppy Canary. The Lancashire was a very large crested variety, with an upright stance, which was required to show no dark plumage whatsoever. At one time the breed 'died out', possibly due to its excessive use in studs of Crested Canaries. Attempts to re-create the breed were made by intermating Yorkshire Canaries and Crested Canaries, and this has been reasonably successful. The appearance of Grizzles within the Gloster

Fancy has been catered for by the provision of one class specifically for Grizzles of the buff-feather type. Grizzles of the yellow-feather type should be exhibited in the appropriate Yellow Corona classes. Grizzles were once far more popular than they are at the present time. Although many people find the total absence of markings very attractive, the mutation tends to be associated with particular characteristics which are not appropriate to a good exhibition Gloster Canary. The main failing tends to be size; generally Grizzles are on the big side and can be excessively long. The markings of many Grizzles improve with age, but as flighted canaries have a tendency to lengthen, any improvement in markings is usually offset by an increase in length.

It is also quite common for Grizzles to be rather upright in their stance and this is another characteristic which is undesirable in exhibition Glosters. Feather quality may also be a problem and quite a large proportion of Grizzles suffer from feather lumps. It is possible to breed Consorts which have grizzled markings, but no special provision is made for these birds in the exhibition classification. Such birds would simply be exhibited in the Buff Consort or Yellow Consort classes, depending on their feather type.

Genetically the Grizzle form is most probably recessive, as it tends to appear quite unexpectedly from time to time. One possible explanation for this phenomenon would be that two birds which both carry the gene for Grizzle hidden in their genetic make-up have, quite by chance, been mated together. The mutation can disappear just as quickly, because if a Grizzle is mated to a bird which does not have the gene for Grizzle in its make-up, no visual Grizzles should be produced. All the young would, however, carry the gene for Grizzle hidden in their genetic make-up and the mutation could reappear if such a bird was mated either to a visual Grizzle or to a bird which carried the Grizzle gene in hidden form. It is also possible to produce White Grizzles and Cinnamon Grizzles, both of which tend to be purely of novelty value.

In the past the practice of mating Grizzle Corona cocks to Three Parts Dark Green Buff Consort hens was recommended in order to produce either Dark Crested Clear Bodied Buffs or Dark Crested Wing Marked Buffs. While this combination could possibly produce the desired markings in its offspring, it must also be remembered that the modern-day exhibition standard for Glosters is more concerned with type, size and feather quality than it is with markings.

Despite their lack of general popularity, good entries of Grizzles can be seen at the larger shows. As recently as 1987, over 50 Grizzles were entered for competition at the IGBA Club Show. However, the same event also boasted an entry of more than 700 Coronas, excluding Grizzles, of which more than 350 were Dark Crested Variegated Green Buffs. Many exhibitors will keep the odd Grizzle, as special prizes are usually offered specifically for these birds at the larger shows.

14   Breeding Pair Selection

In order to produce Gloster Canaries of a consistently good quality, breeders must give very careful consideration to the specific birds that they select to form breeding pairs. Obviously the use of birds which have serious visual faults, no matter what other desirable features they may possess, will undermine the foundations of the stud. Additionally, great caution must be exercised at all times to ensure that birds which are to be mated together are not too closely related. While the mating of very closely related birds may produce visual improvements in the short term, this practice is often the root cause of studs failing to make the grade. Various theories have been advocated over the years about methods whereby breeders are virtually guaranteed to produce top-quality birds if they intermate closely related birds. Most of these theories are flawed and fail to take into account the importance of good, sound, common-sense stockmanship. Various names have been given to some of these theories – In Breeding and Line Breeding, for example – but the allocation of a formal title does nothing to improve their effectiveness.

In Breeding
In Breeding is defined as mating parents to their direct offspring, i.e. father to daughter or mother to son. This method is advocated in order to 'fix' particularly good visual features present in the parent birds in their offspring. Unfortunately, even if this method was not flawed in other respects, it would also be bound to 'fix' all the bad features which may be present. Given that nobody is going to have the luxury of obtaining the best Corona and the best Consort in the whole fancy as their initial stock, it is impossible to produce birds of the desired quality by using this technique.

The ultimate ambition must be to produce birds of the highest possible quality and this cannot be achieved by simply trying to produce 'clones' of the original stock.

Furthermore, the technique totally ignores the fact that genetic flaws are present in virtually all living creatures. These flaws are usually recessive and remain hidden until closely related individuals are intermated. Once two identical errant recessive genes come together, the fault will be manifested in the specimen produced. As the greater part of the appearance, performance and behaviour of all living creatures is related to the genetic information they inherit from their parents, the faults produced may be visual, physical or psychological. While there may seem to be little danger from recessive faults, as they will always be counter-acted by the normal dominant condition, it is these faults that are most difficult to eradicate. This is because recessive faults can be hidden within the genetic make-up of a bird. If imprudent pair selections are made, these faults can spread throughout a whole stud within three or four breeding seasons. Once they are established in a stud of birds, the only way to remove them from your stock is to dispose of all related birds. If methods associated with In Breeding have been employed, this essentially means all your stock. The introduction of unrelated birds may prove to be a stopgap, but sooner or later, and generally it is sooner, the undesirable inherent faults within the stud will reappear once again.

Line Breeding
Line Breeding is defined as the mating together of two individuals which have one parent in common, i.e. half-brother to half-sister. This would be achieved by mating one cock to two different hens and then mating together offspring produced from each mating. In the short term Line Breeding can produce quite promising results, but once again it fails to take account of genetic faults which are bound to be present in the common parent. Even if these faults are not manifested in the first-generation youngsters produced, virtually all will carry the faults hidden in their genetic make-up. Sooner or later these faults will become apparent and the stud will reach a dead end, with breeders finding that at least one particular undesirable characteristic is present in a large

proportion of their stud. The faults manifested can be quite diverse and may include infertility, blindness, madness, hyperactivity, feather problems, lack of vigour, reduced resistance to disease, foot disorders, failure to rear young, heart failure, liver disorders, etc.

The fact that Line Breeding may produce useful results initially should not be regarded as a recommendation for this practice. Often the promising results stem from the fact that the bird used as the common parent was originally outcrossed to two unrelated birds, in order to produce youngsters for half-brother to half-sister matings. The use of unrelated stock tends to reduce the chances of two identical errant genes coinciding in the same individual specimen. Therefore any initial success is more often a recommendation of the value of outcrosses rather than Line Breeding. Persevering with the matings between closely related birds, as recommended by the theory of Line Breeding, will increase the frequency of errant recessive genes. This diminishes the possibility of the errant genes being modified by normal genes, which is the natural method of suppressing the symptoms of genetic disorders.

Planning Ahead

Even if a breeder does not actively follow systems such as In Breeding and Line Breeding, there is a tendency for birds within an individual stud to become too closely related. There are two possible ways to prevent this problem occurring in the first place, and both rely on a steadfast refusal to intermate very closely related birds.

One solution is gradually to build up numbers with a view to eventually maintaining a very large stud of birds. With careful planning and forethought, it should be possible to have available many choices of mate for individual birds each season. However, a large stud on its own is not enough to ensure that a suitably diverse gene pool will always be available. The pedigree of the birds to be used in each pairing must be carefully studied, as must the pedigrees of any young that might be produced from the intended pairings, to ensure that the stud as a whole is not becoming too closely interrelated. When a large stud has been properly established, using birds of the appropriate quality, type and size, it should be possible to select pairings by simply studying the pedigrees of each bird. Visual assessment of stock is only necessary to select those birds which are to be retained for breeding purposes. Once this has been done, provided a few basic rules such as mating Corona to Consort, not mating two white ground birds together and introducing yellow-feathered birds on a regular basis, are observed, the only factor that will determine which specific birds can be mated together is their relationship to each other. If there is a large variation in the visual characteristics of specific birds maintained within one stud, then this indicates that the strain is not true breeding and unsuitable stock has been used in the formative years.

An alternative option is to maintain a smaller stud and rely on the occasional introduction of good-quality, unrelated stock to prevent birds becoming too closely related. In theory this might seem to be the easier of the two options, but in fact it is much more difficult than it sounds. Once a breeder has established a reputation for producing top-quality birds, he or she will often find that birds which would normally be offered for sale are suddenly unavailable if interest is shown in making a purchase. Perhaps the seller lacks confidence in his or her own judgement and thinks that some secret feature that is going to produce top-quality offspring has been overlooked. In truth all the buyer is looking for is a bird of reasonable quality which will help to maintain some diversity of the gene pool within his or her stud.

If you are going to rely on bringing in unrelated birds from time to time, it is essential to build up reliable contacts within the fancy. Provided there is a common bond of trust, this should allow fanciers to swap birds when it is mutually convenient. If you always try to get the best of the deal when swapping birds, offers to make exchanges in the future are very unlikely to be accepted. The system of swapping birds can work only if both parties realize that they must be prepared to part with a good-quality bird in order to obtain a good-quality bird. Successful swaps can usually be made only between fanciers of an equal status; a raw beginner cannot expect an established champion to be interested in making a swap.

In order to exchange birds with any degree of confidence,

A Heavily Variegated Buff Corona hen which was Best Gloster Canary at the Scottish National. The record number of this bird is 5619 and it was bred in 1985. The parents of this bird were 5154 and 5196, which feature in the pedigree sheet for the Cinnamon Buff Consort hen, record number 6368 (see p.184).

you must have first-hand knowledge about the quality of birds maintained by the person with whom the swap is to be made. Not only must you have seen their exhibition stock, you must also be familiar with their breeding stock. Just as there is little point in purchasing birds from a stud which contains birds of a wide variety of different styles, there is no point making exchanges for birds produced by such a stud.

You should always acquire stock from studs where attention has been paid to all the essential characteristics of the breed, and not just to one or two particularly 'eye-catching' features. Furthermore, swaps cannot usefully be made between the same two parties year after year, as this will result in the two studs effectively becoming one large interrelated stud.

By very careful planning it is possible to keep a reasonably small stud fairly unrelated, but this relies heavily on the ability of the breeder to keep just one or two individuals from each pairing. Many people find this impossible for several different reasons. Partly it is because nobody can be certain that a specific bird will breed successfully and therefore 'reserves' need to be retained. Breeders are also reluctant to part with birds which are better visually than those which they must retain in order to prevent their stud becoming too closely related. And many fanciers are terrified of letting good specimens leave their birdroom in case this allows fellow competitors to improve the standard of their studs. In truth, breeders must concentrate on their own stud of birds and not worry unduly about the competition. Provided your own strain improves gradually year by year, progress is being made. Sudden dramatic improvements in the quality of birds being produced tend to be short term and it is more than likely that a sharp improvement will be followed by an equally swift decline.

Practical Considerations
The precise methods adopted by each individual breeder depend very much on their own personal circumstances. There is no merit in keeping a large stud of birds if this means they will be kept in overcrowded conditions or that insufficient time is available to cater for their proper day-to-day management. Breeders must realize that there is no substitute for hard work and the task of producing quality birds first and foremost demands perseverance, dedication and attention to detail. No amount of theorizing and paperwork will compensate for a deficit in these essential ingredients.

15 Records

In order to breed any type of pedigree stock it is essential to keep accurate records of all livestock produced. These records must be easily compiled but at the same time contain sufficient information so that all the required details will be available for future breeding seasons.

Cage Record Cards

The first record card to be maintained is a cage card which can be attached to each breeding cage. This card will need to accommodate details of the individual birds used as parents in this specific cage, a progress report on breeding activities of the pair and details of all the youngsters produced from this pairing. If initial stock birds are not rung with a precisely identifiable ring, this should be rectified immediately to prevent the possibility of confusion between birds of similar

Metal split rings as used for Gloster Canaries.

appearance wearing the same coloured rings. For each pairing, a cage card should be made out, noting the ring number of both the cock and the hen. Generally it simplifies matters if two different coloured inks, one for the cock and one for the hen, are used when making out these cards.

There are four main conditions which can occur in all breeding pairs of canaries: Laying, Sitting, Feeding and Problems. Each of these conditions should be allocated a different colour, and by using self-adhesive coloured spots, the cage cards can be marked so that the progress of any individual pair is known at a glance. When youngsters have been successfully reared by a pair of birds, the ring numbers allocated to the young produced should be recorded on the cage card, before the young are removed from the care of their parents.

CAGE RECORD CARD

PROGRESS LAYING SITTING FEEDING PROBLEMS	COCK:
	HEN:
RING NUMBERS OF YOUNG REARED:	

Breeding Progress Record Sheet

It may be convenient to transfer details from each cage record
on to a larger progress record sheet. This will enable the
breeder to see at a glance the progress being made by each
pairing.

BREEDING PROGRESS RECORD SHEET

COCK RING NUMBER	HEN RING NUMBER	EGGS DUE	YOUNG HATCHED	TOTAL REARED	CAGE NUMBER	REMARKS

Breeding Register

Having recorded the required information on a cage card, you should transfer the information relating to the specific youngsters produced by each pairing to a breeding register. A breeding register needs to contain details of the parent birds used and details of all the youngsters they produce. This information can be taken from the cage record cards and, once this has been done, a new cage card can be used for the next round of youngsters produced by that pairing.

BREEDING REGISTER PAGE

PAIR NO:		YEAR:	
COCK: RING NUMBER: DESCRIPTION:		HEN: RING NUMBER: DESCRIPTION:	

YOUNG PRODUCED:

RING NUMBER	DESCRIPTION	NOTES

ADDITIONAL NOTES:

Keeping records as young birds are rung is essential for any stud.

Pedigree Sheets

Once the birds that will be retained for the following breeding season have been selected, a detailed pedigree sheet for each bird should be completed. Ideally a pedigree sheet will include ring numbers and descriptions of the five previous generations used to produce each bird retained.

Obviously, when you are first starting in the fancy, a large part of the details regarding previous generations will not be known, but it is surprising just how quickly more and more details can be recorded. Failure to keep proper records in the early years can easily cause confusion in the future. Examination of pedigree sheets when making pair selection for the forthcoming breeding season is of great assistance in preventing birds becoming too closely interbred and also in ensuring that yellow-feathered birds are used with sufficient frequency in all pairings. Recording these details can be very time consuming by conventional methods, but with the increased use of home computers it is possible to update quite detailed records relatively easily and quickly. Examples of specific pedigree sheets for birds featured in this book are located on pp. 173–85.

Additional Records
Exhibitors may also like to keep records of the individual show performance of each bird exhibited or details as to where surplus stock has been sold. Exhibition records can be recorded in a separate file or on pedigree sheets, while details about the disposal of stock are usually most easily incorporated into the breeding register.

The fact that accurate records are maintained by no means guarantees that a breeder will be successful in producing good-quality stock. However, a good system of records should prevent stupid mistakes being made when selecting individual birds to form breeding pairs. Furthermore, accurate records will help breeders determine those policies which have been successful in producing good-quality stock and those which have not.

16   Exhibition Standards and Procedures

In order for any type of bird to be exhibited competitively certain criteria must be laid down by those responsible for organizing each particular fancy. If just a few birds of one species are being exhibited, judgements of birds can often be based solely on the condition and presentation of each exhibit and comparisons between different species can be made by taking into account the degree of difficulty in staging a particular species. When many birds of the same species are being exhibited it is necessary to be rather more precise about the shape and style that are felt to be desirable. Should the species become even more popular, new mutations may be developed or different opinions as to what should be the ideal shape and size may arise. If the new mutations or new 'ideals' receive sufficient popular support, a new fancy will emerge from the original species.

Standard of Excellence

In canaries this process has been in operation for many years, so that from one basic species, more than ten different exhibition fancies have developed. Some depend on the presence of an 'unusual' characteristic, such as a crest or frill which is normally absent; others simply develop because enough people prefer birds of a different style or shape to that which was originally envisaged. So that exhibitors know as precisely as possible the ideals they should strive to achieve, and judges are able to determine which features are to be rewarded and which are not, it is necessary in the first place to draw up a written standard which describes the imaginary 'ideal'. The success of each fancy is very dependent on the general acceptance of the written standard.

The present-day exhibition standard in the UK is as follows:

CORONA:	Neatness, regular, unbroken round shape, eye discernible	15 points
	With definite centre	5 points
	OR	
CONSORT:	Head broad and round at every point with good rise over centre of skull	15 points
	Eyebrow heavy, showing browiness	5 points
BODY:	Back well filled, and wings laying closely thereto, full neck, chest nicely rounded without prominence	20 points
TAIL:	Closely folded and well carried	5 points
PLUMAGE:	Close, firm, giving a clean cut appearance, of good quality and natural colour	10 points
CARRIAGE:	Alert, with quick, lively movement	15 points
LEGS AND FEET:	Medium length without blemish	5 points
SIZE:	For the tendency to the diminutive	15 points
CONDITION:	Health and cleanliness	10 points
	TOTAL	100 points

This is an excellent standard with very little room for misinterpretation; the essential features of the breed are protected by being incorporated in the standard and not too much emphasis is placed on any single feature. It can be extremely damaging for a standard to be open to misinterpretation, or if certain features are ignored by particular sections of the fancy. At best this will lead to confusion and disillusion. At worst it could lead to breakaway groups being formed which, in the short term at least, would be detrimental to the overall strength of the fancy.

Pictorial Ideal
In addition to the written standard of excellence, the Gloster Convention has also adopted a set of drawings, produced by Mr C. E. Minjoodt, which give a pictorial representation of the written standard. The danger with pictorial standards is

that they can often become outdated as the fancy progresses and they are all too frequently the subject of revision. This has not been the case with these drawings, which have stood the test of time very well indeed. Provided drawings give a good representation of the 'ideal', they are very useful in helping fanciers, particularly beginners, to imagine the visual interpretation of the written standard. Before anyone can hope to be consistently successful either as an exhibitor or as a judge of any type standard bird, he or she must be able to create an accurate mental picture of the ideal which he or she is seeking to achieve.

Standard Show Cage

In order to exhibit any form of type standard bird, not only is it necessary to have a written exhibition standard, but standards must also be drawn up with respect to exhibition cages. This is necessary so that all birds are exhibited in similar conditions and also ensures that the birds are benched in a cage which complements the breed being exhibited.

A standard Gloster Canary show cage.

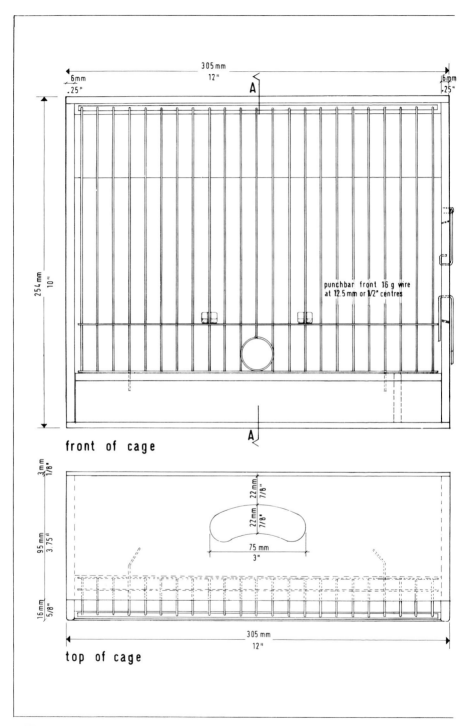

Fig. 7
Plans of the Gloster Fancy Canary standard show cage, produced by Mr C. E. Minjoodt.

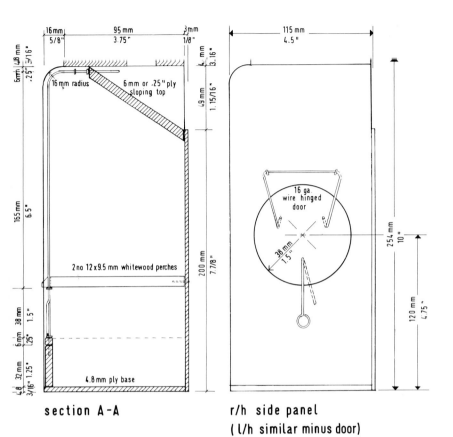

16mm
5/8"

95 mm
3.75"

3mm
1/8"

4 mm
3.16"

6mm
.25"

6mm
.25"

16 mm radius

6mm or .25" ply
sloping top

49 mm
1.15/16"

165 mm
6.5"

200 mm
7.7/8"

2 no 12 x 9.5 mm whitewood perches

38 mm
1.5"

6 mm
.25"

32 mm
1.25"

4.8
3/16"

4.8 mm ply base

section A-A

115 mm
4.5"

16 ga.
wire hinged
door

38 mm
1.5"

254 mm
10"

120 mm
4.75"

r/h side panel
(l/h similar minus door)

CUTTING LIST

3 mm ply	back	305 x 200 mm [12" x 7.7/8"]
4.8 mm ply	top	305 x 95 mm [12" x 3.3/4"]
	bottom	305 x 111 mm [12" x 4.3/8"]
6 mm ply	sides - 2no	244 x 111 mm [9.5/8" x 4.3/8"]
	divider	104 x 38 mm [4.1/8" x 1.1/8"]
	sloping top [angled edges]	293 x 90 mm [11.1/2" x 3.1/2"]
2no perches		12 x 9.5mm [1/2" x 3/8"] softwood 115mm [4.1/2"] long with one splayed end and pin into back

An important feature of the standard Gloster Canary show cage is that the positioning of the perches acts as a means of measuring the overall length of any bird placed in the cage. Ideally, when a Gloster Canary is standing on one perch facing the end of the cage nearest to that perch, its tail should not extend beyond the opposite perch. All black, exterior drinkers are always used on Gloster show cages and the cage label should be positioned on the left-hand side of the front rail, i.e. the opposite end to the door. The floor covering to be used for show cages is seed.

Classification

Having determined the ideal standard for the birds and the specifications of the standard show cage, it is then necessary to draw up an exhibition classification which is appropriate to the fancy. Ideally this should cater adequately for the most popular forms of the breed, but not provide an excessive number of classes for the forms less commonly bred and exhibited. The standard classification for Gloster Canaries, as accepted by the Gloster Convention, provides 25 classes in both the Champion and Novice sections and is as follows:

Flighted Buff Dark Crest Corona Cock
Flighted Buff Dark Crest Corona Hen
Flighted Buff Consort Cock
Flighted Buff Consort Hen
Unflighted Buff Dark Crest Corona Cock
Unflighted Buff Dark Crest Corona Hen
Unflighted Buff Consort Cock
Unflighted Buff Consort Hen
Flighted Buff Three Parts Dark to Self Corona Cock
Flighted Buff Three Parts Dark to Self Corona Hen
Flighted Buff Three Parts Dark to Self Consort Cock
Flighted Buff Three Parts Dark to Self Consort Hen
Unflighted Buff Three Parts Dark to Self Corona Cock
Unflighted Buff Three Parts Dark to Self Corona Hen
Unflighted Buff Three Parts Dark to Self Consort Cock
Unflighted Buff Three Parts Dark to Self Consort Hen
Flighted or Unflighted Yellow Dark or Grizzle Corona Cock
Flighted or Unflighted Yellow Dark or Grizzle Corona Hen

Flighted or Unflighted Yellow Consort Cock
Flighted or Unflighted Yellow Consort Hen
Flighted or Unflighted Yellow or Buff Cinnamon Corona
    Cock or Hen
Flighted or Unflighted Yellow or Buff Cinnamon Consort
    Cock or Hen
Flighted or Unflighted White or Allied to White Corona
    Cock or Hen
Flighted or Unflighted White or Allied to White Consort
    Cock or Hen
Flighted or Unflighted Buff Clear or Grizzle Corona Cock
    or Hen

In addition to these classes a minimum of two classes, one for Coronas and one for Consorts, must be provided for Junior exhibitors.

An examination of the basic 25 classes provided for both Champions and Novices will show that some of the terminology may need to be explained more fully to beginners. Flighted birds are those which are over a year old, having moulted out their flight and tail feathers. Unflighted birds are those bred during the current year which will normally still retain their first set of flight and tail feathers until the following season when they experience their first full moult. Flighted classes are solely for flighted birds and unflighted classes are solely for unflighted birds. Exhibitors do not have the option of entering unflighted birds in flighted classes, or vice versa.

The first eight classes, which are all described as being for buffs are in fact for Clear or Variegated buffs which are neither Cinnamons nor Whites. The next eight classes are for buff-feathered birds which are neither Cinnamons nor Whites and are at least Three Parts Dark (75 per cent non-variegated plumage) or darker. In some birds it may be difficult to decide whether or not a bird is a Variegated or a Three Parts Dark. In such cases, exhibitors can run the risk of having their birds wrong classed, but as no points are awarded for the extent of markings in Gloster Canaries, most enlightened judges will wrong class a bird only if it is very obvious that it is actually in the wrong class.

The four classes for yellows cater for birds of this feather type which are neither Cinnamon nor White. The two Cinnamon classes cater for all normal Cinnamons whether they be buffs or yellows. The two White and Allied to White classes cater for all birds of the White mutation whether they are Clear Whites, Variegated Whites, Blues (white ground Darks) or Fawns (white ground Cinnamons). The final class caters for buff-feathered birds which have a Clear or Grizzle crest, rather than a Dark Crest. The vast majority of Gloster Coronas have a Dark Crest.

Exhibition Status

The definition of exhibition status, in the Gloster Fancy, is generally as follows:

- A Novice is a novice for five years from first joining a Gloster Specialist Club irrespective of First Prizes he or she may be awarded.
- After five years he or she will become a champion (this rule also applies to a Juvenile exhibiting in novice classes).
- Members of the same family residing in the same house shall show under the highest status, with the exception of Juniors.
- A Novice may exhibit in any Gloster classes without affecting his status, if no Novice Classes are provided and entry forms are marked 'novice'.
- Junior membership is from eight to sixteen.

An exception to this may concern juniors residing in the same house as exhibitors of a higher status, where some societies may insist that they show at the highest status in the household.

It can be seen from the definition of a novice and champion exhibitor that the term champion does not necessarily relate to the quality of birds maintained; it simply relates to an exhibitor's length of service in the fancy. Naturally many champion exhibitors will maintain good-quality birds, but this is by no means a foregone conclusion. The purpose of the novice period is to allow beginners to gain a little experience before having to compete directly against well-established exhibitors.

Entering Exhibits

Before exhibiting any birds it is necessary to enter them correctly at an appropriate show. The first thing to do is to obtain a show schedule and entry form. These are usually supplied by the show secretary of the promoting society. When making a request in writing remember to enclose a stamped addressed envelope for the return of the schedule. In addition to other basic information, a show schedule lists all the classes provided at the show and gives details of special awards and prizes offered for competition; it also contains details of patronages granted by other clubs to this particular event. Other details to look for are the venue of the show, the times at which you can bench birds and the lifting time, when you will be allowed to remove your birds from the show.

The entry form should be completed carefully, ensuring birds are entered in the correct section, i.e. Champion, Novice or Junior, and also in the correct classes. Any nominations for specialist societies to which you belong that are offering their special awards for competition should also be clearly marked on your entry form. If birds are being entered in classes containing both flighted and unflighted birds, it is often necessary to state on the entry form whether the birds are flighted or unflighted. If cocks and hens are exhibited in the same class, it may be necessary to state whether the birds entered are cocks or hens, although usually Gloster Canary awards are given to Best in Section and Best Opposite Head, i.e. a Corona if the winner is a Consort, and vice versa, rather than to Best in Section and Best Opposite Sex, as is common in some other sections of the canary fancy. Entry forms should be posted to the show secretary with the correct remittance for your entries and a stamped addressed envelope for the return of your cage labels. People who phone in entries, collect and pay for cage labels on the morning of the show and generally ignore the correct procedures simply cause additional work for show secretaries, who normally have quite enough to do without pandering to the whims of inconsiderate exhibitors. A typical completed entry form may appear as follows:

Class No.	Secs. use only	Description of Exhibit	Nominations	Selling price
197		Unf. Buff Corona Ck	IGBA	NFS
204		Ftd TPD Consort Hn	IGBA	£7.00
206		Unf. TPD Corona Hn	IGBA	NFS
212		Unf. Yellow Consort Hn	IGBA	NFS
215		Ftd Blue Corona Hn	IGBA	NFS

The initials NFS in the selling price column are used to indicate the exhibits are not for sale. Ftd represents Flighted, Unf. represents Unflighted, Ck denotes Cock and Hn is for hen.

A few days before the show exhibitors will receive their cage labels and these may also be accompanied by a lifting card. The lifting card should be kept safe and taken with you to the show so that you can claim your exhibits at lifting time. If lifting cards are not issued it is wise to make a note of your cage labels for your own personal reference.

The Purpose of Competitive Exhibition
While it is very pleasing to win prizes with your birds by exhibiting them, the main purposes of the exercise should not be forgotten. Competitive exhibition is the only accurate way of assessing the progress you have made in trying to attain the imaginary ideal. If you exhibit birds they can be compared directly to exhibits staged by other fanciers and this allows you to see exactly which features of your own stock require improvement. Additionally, being part of the exhibition fancy can be both interesting and stimulating, giving the breeder an ultimate goal at which to aim and also creating the opportunity to meet and talk to other fanciers who share a common interest.

17 Exhibition Preparation

Being able to breed good-quality birds is not enough on its own to make a successful exhibitor. Only if the birds are properly prepared and presented can their owner expect them to realize their full potential on the show bench.

Initial Selection

With the Gloster Canary there are two distinct birds which will be bred and exhibited by fanciers – the Corona and the Consort. While Consorts generally develop quite satisfactorily when kept in relatively large groups in flights or aviaries, employing similar management techniques for Coronas can be disastrous. The first selection of Coronas should be made when they are in nest feather at about three or four weeks of age, and any birds which appear to have exhibition potential at that age should be noted, before being transferred into larger flight units. In order that these birds can be recognized later in the season it is important that they are rung with a numbered identity ring. Provided Coronas are not housed with Consorts, they can usually be kept in their flight units until about the middle of summer without too much damage occurring.

As young birds come through the moult, those which are showing promise should be removed from the flight cages and housed in twos or threes in stock cages. Each identity ring should then be checked against the original notes which were made when the birds were in nest feather. If birds which were noted at this time are missing from the selection, they will need to be located and moved into stock cages. Separating these birds gives them the best possible chance of developing to their full potential.

Eventually all the Coronas bred should be removed from the flight cages and housed in smaller units. The features to look for at this time are shortness in overall length and full, round type or shape. The tail and wings should be neat and tidy and the birds must move well, having a good, lively action, without being flighty. The crests will not be fully developed at this time, so it will be impossible to assess them accurately. The feature to look for is a good definite centre to the crest, which has feathering radiating from the centre equally in all directions.

Training
Once young canaries are housed in groups of two or three, they can be given a little show training. It is most important that birds are handled very gently and carefully during their initial show training. Any clumsiness or impatience on the part of the breeder will result in the birds' confidence being destroyed. Show cages for training purposes should be prepared by covering the floor with coarse sawdust, placing some special treat such as condition seed in the seed box, and positioning a show cage drinker containing fresh water correctly on the front of the cage. Individual birds can then be caught up and placed in these cages for a short period, allowing them to find their way round this 'new environment'.

A great deal of the steadiness of birds in show cages comes from their parentage: flighty birds usually produce flighty youngsters, while those which are confident and steady tend to produce youngsters which are much more easily trained. Legally, in the UK, birds must not be kept in a show cage for more than one hour in any 24-hour period, except for the purposes of competitive exhibition. Therefore any birds which do not take naturally to the show cage must be given additional training by attaching a show cage with an open door to the front of the stock cage: this will allow the birds to enter as they please. If some titbit is placed in the cage, the birds will be encouraged to enter the cage of their own accord and will therefore gain confidence. When birds are placed in show cages, they must be allowed to find the perches in their own time: trying to drive them on to the perches often forces them on to the cage wires, destroying their natural confidence. Cages must be handled very carefully and deliberately during initial show training. Quick or unexpected movements will also be detrimental to the confidence of the birds. Do not rush up to training cages, rattle the cage wires with your fingernails, or poke at the birds with a judging stick. Approach carefully and allow the birds to show themselves naturally, in their own time.

Spraying and Baths

During the show training period, birds will usually be coming through the moult and it is essential that all birds, including flighted birds, are given the opportunity to bathe at least once a week, and more often if at all possible. It is also necessary to spray all potential show birds with water at least twice a week, as this helps to promote good feather condition and displays feather quality to best advantage. The birds should be sprayed thoroughly all over, with Coronas receiving additional spraying on the crest. Do not use too much force when spraying birds as this will startle them and result in a loss of confidence. The water used can be quite warm, as it cools rapidly during spraying, and various proprietary additives such as Plumespray can be added to the water from about two weeks before the first show. For the smaller stud it may be advisable to use a separate cage for spraying birds, to prevent the stock cages becoming excessively damp. However, this is generally impractical in a larger

Pressure sprays are essential in the preparation of exhibition canaries.

stud as it tends to be too time-consuming to catch, spray and replace each bird on a regular basis. It is very important that the birdroom is well ventilated and that cleaning of cages is not neglected when birds are being sprayed so frequently. Any laxity in this respect will result in the birds becoming dirty and the atmosphere of the birdroom being unhealthy. It can also cause rot to develop in the fabric of the birdroom.

Hand-washing

The practice of hand-washing exhibition canaries is quite widespread in certain sections of the fancy but is perhaps not so popular with Gloster Canaries. Occasional hand-washing can be of benefit to your birds if it is properly done, but it should not be undertaken unless you are confident of being able to do the job properly and efficiently. The recommended procedure is as follows.

Bring the full show team and reserves into the house and allow them to settle for at least 30 minutes. Cover cage floors with deep sawdust and place a titbit in the seed box. Prepare a large bowl and two smaller bowls containing warm water. To the large bowl add enough mild shampoo to build up a moderate lather and to the second bowl add a shake of household malt vinegar, to break down the soap from the first bowl. Also required is a very soft and well-used shaving brush and a small cup.

Take a bird to be washed and lower it tail first into the large bowl of water until just the head is above the water. Remove the bird and brush gently, using the shaving brush, always from head to tail. First brush the back, then the wings, then turn the bird and brush the front, flanks and feet. Brush the head last of all. With Coronas always brush in the direction of growth from the centre to the edges and ensure the brush is not too wet.

After brushing, remove any excess soapy water using the side of your finger as a light squeegee. Immerse the finger-dried bird up to its neck in the second bowl, the one containing warm water and a little vinegar. Lift the bird and carefully pour the vinegar water, using the small cup, over the head to remove the soapy water. Finger-dry the bird and then repeat the rinsing process in the third bowl, which contains clean, clear, warm water, and finger dry once again.

Wrap the bird in a strip of towelling so that just the beak protrudes and leave for one minute. After this place the bird in a cage in a warm room at about 70-75°F (21-24°C) and ensure there is plenty of light. The birds must not be allowed to roost until they are fully dried.

The following morning the birds can be returned to the birdroom. Hand-washing should be performed about five days before the show for which birds are to be entered and the whole procedure, from being immersed in the first bowl of water to being removed from the towelling roll and placed in a cage to dry, should not take longer than three minutes in total. If it takes longer than this the birds are being placed under undue stress.

During the time between hand-washing and show day, the show team should be given a very plain diet of canary seed, water and grit. A richer diet can often make the birds very loose in their droppings and negate any advantage gained by the hand-washing procedure.

The final treatment between hand-washing and exhibiting the birds should be a very, very fine, light spray, given on the morning of the day before the show. No bird should be hand-washed more than twice in any one show season.

Dressing

For the eager exhibitor, there is often a temptation to force the natural order of things and start removing odd pin feathers, so that birds can be exhibited this week rather than next week. It is a great mistake to remove or brush out these small wax-covered feathers, as you will then be unable to see the completed specimen with its full complement of feathers for the rest of the season.

With Gloster Canaries, and especially Coronas, it is often thought that a bird's final show appearance depends more on its owner's 'hairdressing' ability than on his or her breeding ability. This is a serious misconception. Gloster Canaries can be regarded as good-quality birds only if they are bred to be good, not made to be good. Practices such as the removal or clipping of tail and wing feathers are not to be condoned and should not be tolerated. It would be foolish to pretend that some Gloster Canaries cannot be improved by the removal of the odd feather. But the emphasis is on the odd feather, and this will usually be a very tiny feather, somewhere in the base of the crest, which slightly displaces the top crest feathers. Even though a bird may be improved by the removal of one feather, remember it can also be ruined if the wrong feather is removed. The general rule is simple: if it can be seen that a bird's plumage has been 'doctored' then it will be penalized; if you can't see any evidence of 'doctoring' the bird will escape penalty. Should you decide that one of your birds will have its chances of success on the show bench improved by a slight adjustment, be extremely careful. You could well put it right out of contention.

Exhibition Equipment
When benching an exhibit, it is not just the bird which will be assessed by the judge. The cage in which the bird is staged is equally important. It should comply to the standards laid down by the Gloster Convention and must be clean and

A smart, tidy carrying case puts the finishing touch to any team of good-quality exhibition Glosters.

properly painted. Exteriors of cages can be polished prior to each show, but remember to put the polish on the cloth and do not spray the polish directly on to the cage. While interior paintwork should be clean and fresh, it can be a disadvantage to have too high a gloss finish on the inside of the cage. This can act as a mirror, allowing the bird to see its own reflection in the back of the cage and causing some birds to spend their time looking at their reflection and away from the judge. If the judge can see only the back of the bird there is no option but to penalize it.

Perches should be fitted properly, always clean, of a uniform size as laid down by the show standards, and made of decent-quality wood, not just from any old scraps which happen to be lying around. Equally important is the condition of carrying boxes. These should be kept clean and tidy, smartly painted, properly ventilated and all fixtures and fittings checked regularly to ensure they are in good order. There is little point spending weeks painstakingly preparing birds for the show bench and then putting them in a carrying box whose handle drops off the first time it is lifted containing its full complement of cages.

Selecting the Show Team
As birds progress through the moult, it will become apparent whether they have the potential to make useful exhibition specimens. Do not rush to get birds on to the show bench too quickly. Early shows can be a great strain on birds if they have not completed their moult, and they can easily go into a 'soft moult' by being exhibited too soon. Should this occur affected birds must not be exhibited again until they have completely recovered, which usually takes at least eight weeks. Do not be tempted to include birds in the show team which have not quite finished the moult just to make up numbers. Give your birds the best possible chance of success by benching them when they are ready, not just because you have two empty show cages. Remember, it is difficult enough to win on the show bench when your birds are in perfect condition, without giving them the immediate handicap of being not fully moulted out.

Going to the Show

Always allow ample time to put up the required birds for exhibition. Before a single bird is placed in a show cage, ensure that all the cages required for the particular show are properly prepared and the drinkers are clean and in good order. The show cage floor should be amply covered with clean, fresh seed and the feeder hopper will usually contain a richer mixture, including condition seed. This gives the birds the 'treat' they always receive on entering a show cage. Cage labels should be attached to the left-hand side of the front rail, when the cage is viewed from the front, and should be straight and tidy. Try to avoid collecting cage labels on the morning of the show and sticking them on while attempting to book the birds into the show.

Once all the cages are properly prepared, the exhibitors can start to place the chosen birds into the appropriate cage. This must be done carefully so that the birds are not distressed or placed in the wrong cage. Always check the show schedule, as birds are being placed in cages, to ensure they are in the correct class. The birds should be allowed water while they are being put up in the birdroom and once all exhibits have been put up and the exhibitor is happy that they are presented to the best of his or her ability, the water can be removed and the cages placed in the carrying case and brought into the house. When the birds have been allowed to settle, the carrying case lids can be lowered and the cases fastened for the night. Ensure that the house temperature is not excessive and that the birds are not positioned close to heaters or radiators. On the morning of the show leave home early enough so that you can arrive on time without rushing and driving recklessly. It is often wise to take a spare, clean show cage with you so that, provided you arrive in good time, all exhibits can be checked and any birds which have soiled their cages can be removed, allowing the cage to be cleaned and made presentable. Obviously if you arrive a few minutes before the final benching time you will not be permitted to hold everybody up while attempting to clean a dirty cage.

Returning from the Show

On returning with your exhibits from a show remember that your birds will have experienced quite a number of changes in conditions in a very short space of time and therefore need a little bit of special treatment on their return to the birdroom. All birds which have been exhibited should be sprayed with warm water the morning after they return from the show and given a little bit of rearing food. It is also wise not to return the birds to the birdroom on the evening after a show as the majority of birdrooms tend to be colder than most show halls, and the sudden change in temperature from a show hall on a sunny autumn afternoon to a birdroom on a frosty autumn night can be much too severe and cause the

Nick and Annalain Barrett with the National Exhibition of Cage Birds trophies for Best Gloster Canary, Best Canary, Best Flighted Canary and Best White Canary, all of which were won by the 'Glenariff' stud of birds at the show staged in 1983.

THE GLOSTER FANCY CANARY

birds to go into a soft moult. After each use, show cages must be emptied of all old seed, washed and cleaned, the old cage label must be removed and the show cage drinkers washed out and cleaned. Seed used as covering for show cage floors should not be fed to the birds at a later date, nor should it be used to cover the show cage floor at the next show. Recycling this seed can lead to severe digestive disorders in canaries and the possible consequences are not worth risking for the small sums saved by reusing the seed.

Personal Pride
It is not possible for everyone to own outstanding exhibition birds, but it is possible for everyone to prepare and present their birds in the correct and proper manner on the show bench. The task of ensuring you always exhibit clean and healthy birds, benched in clean and sound cages, should be a matter of personal pride. Any laxity with regard to the manner in which birds are benched not only penalizes the exhibit; it also reflects badly on the fancier responsible for exhibiting the birds.

18 Judging

As a breeder builds up his or her own stud of birds and hopefully becomes more successful on the show bench, thoughts generally turn to judging a Gloster Canary section, rather than exhibiting in the section. The qualifications required to be considered as a Gloster Canary panel judge within the UK are as follows.

- A judge must be a current-year Gloster Breeder and Exhibitor at open shows, with at least five years as a Champion Exhibitor.

In order to become a specialist Gloster Club panel judge, the exhibitor will need to apply formally, in accordance with the rules of the society concerned; details can be obtained from each particular society.

Accepting Invitations

Having become a panel judge, there is very little to be done until you receive your first invitation to officiate at a show. On receiving an invitation you should note carefully the date and location of the show and the sections you are required to judge. Some events invite judges to place awards in more than one section. If you know nothing about the birds in the other section it is pointless accepting the engagement. It is important to reply promptly, in writing, to any request for your services as a judge, whether or not you intend to accept the invitation. Your reply should confirm the date and location of the show, the section or sections you will be expected to judge, details of your expenses and whether or not you will require overnight accommodation. Should you have to travel for more than about 90 minutes in order to reach the show, it may be advisable to request overnight accommodation. Bear in mind that shows are usually held at the worst time of year for travelling conditions. Fog, ice and snow can easily double the expected travelling time, and it is important to arrive at the show promptly, clear-headed and relaxed. Judges who have been driving for three hours immediately before the show will rarely perform to the best of their potential.

Arriving at the Show
Having arrived at the show, judges should introduce themselves to the person who booked their services, usually the show secretary. This person will usually give the judge all the paperwork he or she requires to judge the section, except for a list of absentees, which can be provided only once all the entries have been received on the morning of the show. Having 'reported for duty', examine the paperwork, ensure you have a judging book, list of specials to be awarded and a show schedule. It is often advisable to walk round your section as it is staged in the show hall, before starting judging. You will gain a fair impression of the number and quality of exhibits which have been benched and can make a mental note of any exhibits which 'catch your eye' at this particular time. Judges should expect to start their duties promptly, according to the time given on the show schedule, and if there is any delay, have no reservations about mentioning this fact to the show secretary.

Instructing Stewards
Before anyone can start judging a section he or she must be allocated some stewards and it is important that these people do their job correctly and efficiently. After introducing yourself to your stewards, and remembering their names, explain the basic procedures you wish them to carry out. Discourage any comments about birds while you are actually in the process of placing awards: you have been booked to give your opinion; it is not a team effort. Instruct the stewards never to put any cages on the floor. This will upset birds and exhibitors alike. If you dislike people smoking near birds, tell stewards so that there can be no misunderstanding later. If you smoke yourself, remember not to exhale into the cages you are trying to judge. No bird will perform to its full potential in a cage filled with cigarette smoke.

In addition to a judging bench, you will also require at least one table on which to place your winners after each class is judged. Should you think your judging stand is inadequate – it may be too high for example – or you have nowhere suitable to place your winners, ask a steward to inform the show manager that you wish to complain about your facilities.

Before you start judging each class ensure that all the exhibits entered in the class are present. If there are less than the number indicated in your judging book, check your list of absentees. Should you still not be able to account for all the exhibits entered, the stewards will have to make further enquiries with the show secretary. It is a wise precaution to note the cage numbers of all absentees, just in case they turn up in the show hall after judging is completed. As each class of birds is judged, the winner should be retained, and all other birds returned to the show benches and fully watered. Do not let anyone stand birds from your section near radiators or in draughts, as this will be detrimental to their appearance and physical condition.

Commencing Judging

Once you have issued your instructions and made sure all the necessary paperwork is at hand, you will be ready to start judging the first class. Judge all birds at the same level, i.e. side by side. Do not stand one cage on top of another, as you cannot compare the type of individual birds accurately when looking up at one and down at another. It is also very difficult to assess type accurately if you stand closer than an arm's length from the exhibits. Naturally you must move closer to examine some of the other essential features, but remember to step back when assessing type. There is no need to poke at birds with a judging stick if they do not show themselves properly: it is not the fault of the judge that the birds have not been adequately trained. Nor is there any need to strum the wires of the cage front with your fingernails in order to place birds in the correct order. Allow birds to perform naturally as you assess them, encourage those which are a little static to move by gently working the bird with your hands, so that they move to and fro from perch to perch, and so display their natural action.

Judges must always try to be consistent. You should have birds which are of similar styles taking the awards in classes whenever possible. This can be achieved only by paying particular attention to the type and size of exhibits, ensuring that you are not swayed by one individual feature, such as crest length or width of head. Do not ask for anyone else's opinion: the judge judges the birds; everyone else judges the judge. Having placed the exhibits in what you believe to be the appropriate order, mark up the cage labels, first to seventh in each class, and record the result on your judging slip, making sure these are correct. When a judging slip is completed (often two classes make up one slip) sign it, remove it from the judging book and instruct your steward to return it to the show secretary.

Judges should not be overawed when faced with large classes containing 40 or 50 exhibits. These classes are no more difficult to judge than small classes, provided you ensure that you actually see all the birds which have been entered in the class. Simply eliminate exhibits until you are left with the best eight or nine in the class, so that you can determine the first seven placings. In large classes, dirty cages, perches and birds can be eliminated immediately, as can birds with nails and claws missing. Next tackle birds which lack condition, those which are too big and any which display the wrong shape. If you are confronted with birds that seem to have been 'dressed', but you are not sure, remember that as a judge you have the right to handle any exhibit placed before you, to check for possible malpractice. Inform the show manager before you start catching up birds, and make sure he or she is in attendance when you handle an exhibit. If you find it difficult to choose between two very similar out-standing exhibits, especially if your decision will probably permit one of the birds to go on and take a Best in Section award, take a break from looking at these birds for a few minutes before making your final decision.

Selecting Specials Winners
After all the classes, including the Junior section, have been judged, the judge must allocate his or her section specials. This can be quite complicated, but adhering to a few basic procedures will help to eliminate mistakes. The first step is to

Nick Barrett with the exhibit which won Best in Show, Best Unflighted Exhibit and Best Champion Exhibit at the 1987 IGBA Club Show. This particular event attracted an entry in excess of 1,800 Gloster Canaries, which is the highest entry of Glosters recorded at one show to date. The bird that won on this occasion was an Unflighted Three Parts Dark Buff Corona hen.

take all the first-prize winners from a section, i.e. Champion, Novice or Junior, and divide these into Coronas and Consorts. Then judge all the winners of the Champion Corona classes, as one class, at least down to seventh place. (At larger events they may need to be judged down to thirteenth place.) Now record your placings. Repeat the process with the Champion Consorts, judging first to seventh, or twelfth, as appropriate. Comparing the Best Corona and the Best Consort, and deciding which is the better exhibit, will mean the Best Champion Exhibit has been found. Repeating the process with the Novice classes and the Junior classes will produce the Best Novice Exhibit and the Best Junior Exhibit. When the three Best in Section Exhibits are compared, the Best Gloster award can be allocated.

As the best bird in each section is selected, all the special awards it is qualified to receive should be allocated. For example, if the Best Champion Exhibit is an Unflighted Buff Corona hen, it must automatically win the awards for Best Champion Buff, Best Champion Corona and Best Champion Unflighted, if these awards are on offer. If the Best Champion Consort is a Flighted Three Parts Dark cock, it will obviously be Best Champion Consort and Best Champion Opposite Head, but not necessarily Best Champion Three Parts Dark, or Best Champion Flighted, as it will need to be judged against the appropriate Coronas, in order to place these awards. If you work through your list of specials systematically, you will be able to place all the awards, provided exhibits which are eligible for these awards have been entered. Winners for some awards offered by specialist societies may take a little more finding if only a few of the exhibitors are members of these clubs. But again, by a process of elimination and systematic working these can usually be found without too much difficulty.

On occasion judges may then be asked to judge for Best Canary or Best in Show, although these awards are now becoming less popular. In order to do this you must have more than a passing knowledge of the birds you have been asked to assess. Try and give an honest opinion of the birds placed before you: do not just opt for the bird you have selected from your own section, regardless of the other exhibits. When judging exhibits from different sections, the Best from each section should be represented by just one judge from that section. If the system is not properly organized, complain to the show manager.

Show Standards

While the Gloster Canary has a standard of excellence, with various features being allocated a certain number of points (see p.142), the points really indicate the relative importance of each feature that goes to make up the complete bird. Although only five points are allocated for feet and legs, this does not mean that an exhibit with only one leg loses just two and a half points: obviously such birds must be more heavily penalized. Similarly there are only five points allocated for the tail, but again a bird without a tail must be consigned to the also-rans and not just penalized by five points. When judging Gloster Canaries it is sensible to make some minor allowances for the sex, age and degree of difficulty associated with particular examples of the breed. Hens generally tend to be of a better type than cocks, unflighted birds are generally shorter than flighted birds and Cinnamons rarely exhibit the same quality of type as Normal Buffs. With regard to wrong classing exhibits, there is no need to be too pedantic about whether birds are Buffs or Three Parts Dark; no points are allocated for the distribution of variegated markings and therefore, provided birds are fairly close to the class in which they are exhibited, they need not be wrong classed. There is no need to make excessive comments on cage labels, and this should be done only for the education of exhibitors, generally Novices and Juniors, who may have missed some technical point, such as the thickness or positioning of the show cage perches. Other notes such as birds refusing to perch should be noted by the judge personally, so they can be referred to later in the day, should exhibitors query his or her decisions. Remember, it is the birds which are not placed in the cards that disgruntled exhibitors generally ask judges to reassess on the afternoon of the show, not those which have won awards.

19 Mating Expectations

The following list of mating expectations is not intended to be a comprehensive catalogue of all the matings it is possible to make between different colours of Gloster Canaries. It is simply provided to give breeders a quick reference to some of the commoner matings which might be used to produce birds of a specific colour. The list of matings is laid out in a uniform pattern with the parents used on the left and the young it is possible to produce on the right. Percentages given are based on the results that would be obtained if a very large number of young were produced from a specific pairing. In practice these percentages can vary considerably from nest to nest. In order to represent birds which are 'carrying' colours other than those they display visually the standard oblique stroke is used. The visual appearance of the bird is to the left of the '/' and the colours which are carried in hidden form within the genetic make-up of the bird appear to the right. Thus a Cinnamon Carrier cock appears as Normal/Cinnamon cock.

Recessive Mutations
Virtually all Gloster Canaries carry the gene responsible for producing Variegated birds and, in the majority of cases, they will actually be visual examples of the Variegated mutation. With regard to the genetic classification of birds, all canaries from Clears through to Fouls are Variegateds. The Variegated mutation is in fact recessive and the predominance of these birds illustrates just how easily recessive mutations can become established. Because so many canaries are Variegated, the term Normal, as used in these mating lists, actually refers to birds which are Variegated Greens. The extent and distribution of the variegated markings displayed are of little consequence to the genetic expectations.

Sex-Linked Mutations

Cinnamons are an example of a recessive sex-linked mutation. With this method of inheritance the gene which produces the mutation is located on the X chromosome. Cock birds possess two X chromosomes, while hens have only one X chromosome, which is matched to a Y chromosome. The sole function of the Y chromosome is to determine the sex of the bird produced. Hens will automatically be visual examples of a sex-linked colour if the single X chromosome they inherit contains the gene responsible for producing that mutation. In the case of cock birds, both their X chromosomes must contain this mutant gene before they will be visual examples of the mutation. The results obtained from sex-linked mutations are therefore dependent, not only on the colour of parent birds, but also on whether a cock or hen of the sex-linked mutation is used in matings. Incidentally, in humans the female has two X chromosomes and the male one X and one Y chromosome, the reverse of the situation in birds.

Dominant Mutations

The white ground colour form is an example of a genetically dominant mutation. Basically this is the opposite to a recessive mutation and a dominant mutation cannot be carried hidden in the genetic make-up of a bird. If a bird is going to pass the gene responsible for producing a dominant mutation on to its offspring, it must be a visual example of that mutation. It is often the case that a 'double dose' of a dominant mutation proves to be lethal. This is believed to be the case in both the dominant mutations associated with Gloster Canaries, which are the White mutation and the mutation responsible for producing the Corona or Crest. A bird which is a visual example of a dominant mutation, but carries the Normal gene hidden in its genetic make-up, should really be referred to as a single factor or (s.f.) example of the mutation. Birds which carry two genes for a dominant mutation would be described as double factor or (d.f.) specimens. However, as double factor birds are not viable in the dominant mutations associated with Glosters, these terms are never used in general conversation. The terms s.f. and d.f. are, however, used in the matings listed here, in order to give a more complete picture. Obviously the mating involving a White (d.f.) bird as a parent is purely hypothetical, but demonstrates what would happen if it were possible to breed a double factor bird of a dominant mutation.

Combined Mutations

By producing birds which visually show the characteristics of more than one mutation, it is possible to 'create' additional variety in a stud of canaries. The colour usually referred to as Fawn in canary circles is produced by combining the Cinnamon and the White mutations. Pairings involving Cinnamons and Whites are included in the list of matings so that breeders can either ascertain the most effective methods of producing Fawns, or determine how any Fawns which may crop up unexpectedly have been produced. In order to produce Fawns, however, it is essential that one of the parent birds visually displays the White mutation, in either its Normal or its Cinnamon form.

LIST OF MATINGS AND EXPECTATIONS

Recessive

Self Green × Variegated	→ 100% Green/Variegated
Self Green/Variegated × Self Green/Variegated	→ 25% Self Green, 50% Self Green/Variegated and 25% Variegated
Self Green/Variegated × Variegated	→ 50% Self Green/Variegated and 50% Variegated
Variegated × Variegated	→ 100% Variegated

Sex Linked

Normal Cock × Cinnamon Hen	→ 50% Normal/Cinnamon Cocks and 50% Normal Hens
Normal/Cinnamon Cock × Normal Hen	→ 25% Normal Cocks, 25% Normal/Cinnamon Cocks, 25% Normal Hens and 25% Cinnamon Hens
Normal/Cinnamon Cock × Cinnamon Hen	→ 25% Cinnamon Cocks, 25% Normal/Cinnamon Cocks, 25% Cinnamon Hens and 25% Normal Hens

Cinnamon Cock × Normal Hen	→	50% Normal/Cinnamon Cocks and 50% Cinnamon Hens
Cinnamon Cock × Cinnamon Hen	→	100% Cinnamon Cocks and Hens

Dominant

Normal × White (s.f.)	→	50% Normal and 50% White (s.f.)
White (s.f.) × White (s.f.)	→	25% Normal, 50% White (s.f.) and 25% White (d.f.) [Not viable]
White (d.f.) [Not viable] × Normal	→	100% White (s.f.)

Combined

White (s.f.) Cock × Cinnamon Hen	→	25% White (s.f.)/Cinnamon Cocks, 25% Normal/ Cinnamon Cocks, 25% White (s.f.) Hens and 25% Normal Hens
Cinnamon Cock × White (s.f.) Hen	→	25% White (s.f.)/Cinnamon Cocks, 25% Normal/ Cinnamon Cocks, 25% Cinnamon Hens and 25% Fawn (s.f.) Hens
Cinnamon Cock × Fawn (s.f.) Hen	→	25% Cinnamon Cocks, 25% Fawn (s.f.) Cocks, 25% Cinnamon Hens and 25% Fawn (s.f.) Hens
White (s.f.)/Cinnamon Cock × Cinnamon Hen	→	12½% Normal/Cinnamon Cocks, 12½% Cinnamon Cocks, 12½% White (s.f.)/ Cinnamon Cocks, 12½% Fawn (s.f.) Cocks, 12½% Normal Hens, 12½% Cinnamon Hens, 12½% White (s.f.) Hens and 12½% Fawn (s.f.) Hens
Normal/Cinnamon Cock × Fawn (s.f.) Hen	→	12½% Normal/Cinnamon Cocks, 12½% Cinnamon Cocks, 12½% White (s.f.)/ Cinnamon Cocks, 12½% Fawn (s.f.) Cocks, 12½% Normal Hens, 12½% Cinnamon Hens, 12½% White (s.f.) Hens and 12½% Fawn (s.f.) Hens

Normal/Cinnamon Cock × White (s.f.) Hen → 12½% Normal Cocks, 12½% Normal/Cinnamon Cocks, 12½% White (s.f.)/Cinnamon Cocks, 12½% White (s.f.) Cocks, 12½% Normal Hens, 12½% White (s.f.) Hens, 12½% Cinnamon Hens and 12½% Fawn (s.f.) Hens

Fawn (s.f.) Cock × Cinnamon Hen → 25% Cinnamon Cocks, 25% Fawn (s.f.) Cocks, 25% Cinnamon Hens and 25% Fawn (s.f.) Hens

Fawn (s.f.) Cock × Normal Hen → 25% Normal/Cinnamon Cocks, 25% White (s.f.)/Cinnamon Cocks, 25% Cinnamon Hens and 25% Fawn (s.f.) Hens

Appendix Pedigree Sheets

Included here are six pedigree sheets which relate to certain birds that are shown within the book. The specific pedigree sheets chosen emphasize many of the ideas and opinions expressed within the text of the book. Additional information about the relationship of birds whose pedigree sheets are not included here is given in the captions to photographs.

The reference number given alongside each bird is specific to that bird and is the means by which it is possible to differentiate precisely between birds of similar appearance. Obviously it is impossible to give full descriptions of each individual bird featured on the pedigree sheet. Birds which are not described as being Cinnamon, Blue or Fawn are Green, showing various degrees of variegation. All birds of the white ground mutation are described as Blues, whether they are Lightly Variegated or Three Parts Dark. All the Cinnamons, Blues and Fawns used within the matings are of the buff-feather type. Cocks which carry the gene for Cinnamon hidden within their genetic make-up are additionally described as (cinnamon carrier) or (c.c.). Lightly Variegated birds include clear-bodied, dark-crested Coronas and clear or ticked Consorts. Birds described as Selfs would generally be more correctly described as Self or Foul.

Careful examination of these pedigree sheets should help the breeder to see how a successful stud has been carefully constructed using sound techniques. In order to produce quality birds there has been no need to use matings such as father to daughter, mother to son or half-brother to half-sister.

BREED: **GLOSTER CANARY**

RING NUMBER: **4716**

PARENTS	GRANDPARENTS	GREAT GRANDPARENTS
Sire 3274 Heavily Variegated Buff Corona	Sire 2238 Three Parts Dark Buff Corona	Sire 2174 Variegated Buff Corona
		Dam 2128 Three Parts Dark Buff Consort
	Dam 2591 Three Parts Dark Yellow Consort	Sire 1976 Heavily Variegated Buff Corona
		Dam 2190 Three Parts Dark Yellow Consort
Dam 3727 Three Parts Dark Buff Consort	Sire 1856 Three Parts Dark Buff Corona	Sire 1527 Variegated Buff Corona
		Dam 1597 Three Parts Dark Buff Consort
	Dam 1808 Variegated Buff Consort	Sire 1571 Lightly Variegated Buff Corona
		Dam 1399 Three Parts Dark Buff Consort

DESCRIPTION: THREE PARTS DARK BUFF CORONA HEN

YEAR BRED: 1982

GREAT GREAT GRANDPARENTS	GREAT GREAT GREAT GRANDPARENTS
Sire 1070 Variegated Buff Corona	Sire 1000 Lightly Variegated Buff Consort
	Dam 799 Heavily Variegated Buff Corona
Dam 1867 Three Parts Dark Buff Consort	Sire 1362 Heavily Variegated Buff Consort
	Dam 1637 Variegated Buff Corona
Sire 1559 Three Parts Dark Yellow Corona	Sire 1387 Heavily Variegated Buff Consort
	Dam 1318 Three Parts Dark Yellow Corona
Dam 1687 Variegated Buff Consort	Sire 1483 Variegated Buff Consort
	Dam 1340 Heavily Variegated Buff Corona
Sire 1856 Three Parts Dark Buff Corona	Sire 1527 Variegated Buff Corona
	Dam 1597 Three Parts Dark Buff Consort
Dam 1808 Variegated Buff Consort	Sire 1571 Lightly Variegated Buff Corona
	Dam 1399 Three Parts Dark Buff Consort
Sire 1663 Three Parts Dark Buff Corona	Sire 1070 Variegated Buff Corona
	Dam 1399 Three Parts Dark Buff Consort
Dam 2042 Three Parts Dark Yellow Consort	Sire 1557 Three Parts Dark Yellow Consort
	Dam 916 Heavily Variegated Buff Corona
Sire 1341 Variegated Buff Corona	Sire 1070 Variegated Buff Corona
	Dam 1089 Variegated Blue Buff Consort
Dam 1378 Variegated Buff Consort	Sire 1247 Variegated Buff Consort
	Dam 1333 Variegated Buff Corona
Sire 1398 Three Parts Dark Blue Buff Corona	Sire 1244 Three Parts Dark Blue Consort
	Dam 1136 Heavily Variegated Buff Corona
Dam 1338 Variegated Buff Consort	Sire 1070 Variegated Buff Corona
	Dam 1003 Three Parts Dark Blue Consort
Sire 1483 Variegated Buff Consort	Sire 1258 Lightly Variegated Buff Corona
	Dam 1354 Three Parts Dark Buff Consort
Dam 1340 Heavily Variegated Buff Corona	Sire 1070 Variegated Buff Corona
	Dam 1003 Three Parts Dark Blue Consort
Sire 1244 Three Parts Dark Blue Buff Consort	Sire 1206 Variegated Blue Buff Corona
	Dam 1200 Three Parts Dark Yellow Consort
Dam 1136 Heavily Variegated Buff Corona	Sire 782 Three Parts Dark Blue Consort
	Dam 614 Three Parts Dark Buff Corona

BREED: **GLOSTER CANARY**

RING NUMBER: **5167**

PARENTS	GRANDPARENTS	GREAT GRANDPARENTS
Sire 4701 Three Parts Dark Yellow Consort	**Sire** 4337 Variegated Buff Corona	**Sire** 3547 Heavily Variegated Buff Corona
		Dam 3772 Three Parts Dark Buff Consort
	Dam 4228 Three Parts Dark Yellow Consort	**Sire** 3000 Three Parts Dark Buff Corona
		Dam 3164 Heavily Variegated Yellow Consort
Dam 4966 Variegated Buff Corona	**Sire** 4449 Heavily Variegated Buff Consort	**Sire** 3669 Heavily Variegated Buff Consort
		Dam 3801 Variegated Buff Corona
	Dam 4532 Variegated Buff Corona	**Sire** 3884 Heavily Variegated Buff Corona
		Dam 3544 Lightly Variegated Buff Consort

DESCRIPTION: VARIEGATED BUFF CORONA HEN

YEAR BRED: 1984

GREAT GREAT GRANDPARENTS	GREAT GREAT GREAT GRANDPARENTS
Sire 3121 Heavily Variegated Buff Consort	Sire 2786 Variegated Buff Corona (c.c.)
	Dam 2671 Three Parts Dark Buff Consort
Dam 3143 Heavily Variegated Buff Corona	Sire 2227 Heavily Variegated Buff Consort
	Dam 2977 Three Parts Dark Yellow Corona
Sire 2760 Heavily Variegated Buff Corona	Sire 1976 Heavily Variegated Buff Corona
	Dam 2190 Three Parts Dark Yellow Consort
Dam 1925 Three Parts Dark Buff Consort	Sire 1483 Variegated Buff Consort
	Dam 1563 Three Parts Dark Buff Corona
Sire 2760 Heavily Variegated Buff Corona	Sire 1976 Heavily Variegated Buff Corona
	Dam 2190 Three Parts Dark Yellow Consort
Dam 2862 Three Parts Dark Buff Consort	Sire 2210 Heavily Variegated Buff Consort
	Dam 2110 Three Parts Dark Buff Corona
Sire 2674 Three Parts Dark Buff Corona	Sire 1286 Variegated Buff Consort
	Dam 1825 Three Parts Dark Buff Corona
Dam 2352 Three Parts Dark Yellow Consort	Sire 2025 Three Parts Dark Buff Corona
	Dam 2042 Three Parts Dark Yellow Consort
Sire 2613 Heavily Variegated Buff Consort	Sire 2449 Heavily Variegated Buff Corona
	Dam 2219 Three Parts Dark Buff Consort
Dam 2787 Heavily Variegated Yellow Corona	Sire 2224 Heavily Variegated Buff Corona
	Dam 1719 Three Parts Dark Yellow Consort
Sire 3141 Variegated Buff Corona	Sire 2227 Heavily Variegated Buff Consort
	Dam 2977 Three Parts Dark Yellow Corona
Dam 3029 Heavily Variegated Buff Consort	Sire 2763 Heavily Variegated Yellow Corona
	Dam 2704 Heavily Variegated Buff Consort
Sire 3099 Heavily Variegated Buff Corona	Sire 2803 Three Parts Dark Blue Consort
	Dam 2679 Variegated Buff Corona
Dam 2733 Three Parts Dark Buff Consort	Sire 2208 Heavily Variegated Buff Consort
	Dam 2353 Three Parts Dark Buff Corona
Sire 1914 Lightly Variegated Buff Corona	Sire 1571 Lightly Variegated Buff Corona
	Dam 1399 Three Parts Dark Buff Consort
Dam 2810 Self Buff Consort	Sire 2231 Three Parts Dark Yellow Consort
	Dam 2402 Three Parts Dark Buff Corona

BREED: GLOSTER CANARY

RING NUMBER: 5215

PARENTS	GRANDPARENTS	GREAT GRANDPARENTS
Sire 4777 Three Parts Dark Blue Buff Corona (cinnamon carrier)	Sire 4411 Heavily Variegated Buff Corona	Sire 2449 Heavily Variegated Buff Corona
		Dam 3866 Self Buff Consort
	Dam 4394 Three Parts Dark Fawn Buff Consort	Sire 4121 Three Parts Dark Blue Buff Consort (cinnamon carrier)
		Dam 3591 Heavily Variegated Buff Corona
Dam 4425 Self Buff Consort	Sire 2808 Self Yellow Corona	Sire 2231 Three Parts Dark Yellow Consort
		Dam 2402 Three Parts Dark Buff Corona
	Dam 2797 Heavily Variegated Buff Consort	Sire 2449 Heavily Variegated Buff Corona
		Dam 2219 Three Parts Dark Buff Consort

DESCRIPTION: THREE PARTS DARK BUFF CORONA COCK

YEAR BRED: 1984

GREAT GREAT GRANDPARENTS	GREAT GREAT GREAT GRANDPARENTS
Sire 2058 Heavily Variegated Buff Consort	Sire 1786 Heavily Variegated Buff Consort
	Dam 1635 Heavily Variegated Buff Corona
Dam 1733 Heavily Variegated Buff Corona	Sire 1390 Variegated Buff Corona
	Dam 1630 Heavily Variegated Buff Consort
Sire 3099 Heavily Variegated Buff Corona	Sire 2803 Three Parts Dark Blue Consort
	Dam 2679 Variegated Buff Corona
Dam 3242 Self Yellow Consort	Sire 2808 Self Yellow Corona
	Dam 2359 Three Parts Dark Buff Consort
Sire 3786 Heavily Variegated Blue Buff Corona (c.c.)	Sire 2801 Three Parts Dark Blue Corona
	Dam 80 Three Parts Dark Cinnamon Consort
Dam 3717 Heavily Variegated Buff Consort	Sire 3121 Heavily Variegated Buff Consort
	Dam 3143 Heavily Variegated Buff Corona
Sire 3228 Lightly Variegated Buff Corona	Sire 1838 Variegated Buff Consort
	Dam 2702 Heavily Variegated Buff Corona
Dam 3190 Three Parts Dark Buff Consort	Sire 1976 Heavily Variegated Buff Corona
	Dam 2190 Three Parts Dark Yellow Consort
Sire 1976 Heavily Variegated Buff Corona	Sire 1856 Three Parts Dark Buff Corona
	Dam 1808 Variegated Buff Consort
Dam 2190 Three Parts Dark Yellow Consort	Sire 1663 Three Parts Dark Buff Corona
	Dam 2042 Three Parts Dark Yellow Consort
Sire 1744 Heavily Variegated Buff Corona	Sire 1483 Variegated Buff Consort
	Dam 1563 Three Parts Dark Buff Corona
Dam 2173 Three Parts Dark Buff Consort	Sire 1856 Three Parts Dark Buff Corona
	Dam 1801 Three Parts Dark Cinnamon Consort
Sire 2058 Heavily Variegated Buff Consort	Sire 1786 Heavily Variegated Buff Consort
	Dam 1635 Heavily Variegated Buff Corona
Dam 1733 Heavily Variegated Buff Corona	Sire 1390 Variegated Buff Corona
	Dam 1630 Heavily Variegated Buff Consort
Sire 1976 Heavily Variegated Buff Corona	Sire 1856 Three Parts Dark Buff Corona
	Dam 1808 Variegated Buff Consort
Dam 2190 Three Parts Dark Yellow Consort	Sire 1663 Three Parts Dark Buff Corona
	Dam 2042 Three Parts Dark Yellow Consort

BREED: GLOSTER CANARY

RING NUMBER: 5907

PARENTS	GRANDPARENTS	GREAT GRANDPARENTS
Sire 5440 Three Parts Dark Buff Consort	Sire 5154 Three Parts Dark Buff Consort	Sire 4399 Three Parts Dark Yellow Consort
		Dam 4903 Three Parts Dark Buff Corona
	Dam 5147 Variegated Buff Corona	Sire 3180 Three Parts Dark Buff Consort
		Dam 4431 Variegated Buff Corona
Dam 5469 Three Parts Dark Cinnamon Buff Corona	Sire 4756 Three Parts Dark Fawn Buff Consort	Sire 4200 Three Parts Dark Buff Consort (cinnamon carrier)
		Dam 4564 Three Parts Dark Fawn Buff Corona
	Dam 4903 Three Parts Dark Buff Corona	Sire 3813 Three Parts Dark Buff Consort
		Dam 4605 Three Parts Dark Buff Corona

DESCRIPTION: VARIEGATED BUFF CORONA HEN

YEAR BRED: 1987

GREAT GREAT GRANDPARENTS	GREAT GREAT GREAT GRANDPARENTS
Sire 3288 Heavily Variegated Buff Corona	Sire 2760 Heavily Variegated Buff Corona
	Dam 1925 Three Parts Dark Buff Consort
Dam 3164 Heavily Variegated Yellow Consort	Sire 2674 Three Parts Dark Buff Corona
	Dam 2352 Three Parts Dark Yellow Consort
Sire 3813 Three Parts Dark Buff Consort	Sire 3712 Heavily Variegated Buff Corona
	Dam 3295 Self Buff Consort
Dam 4605 Three Parts Dark Buff Corona	Sire 2449 Heavily Variegated Buff Corona
	Dam 3866 Self Buff Consort
Sire 2613 Heavily Variegated Buff Consort	Sire 2449 Heavily Variegated Buff Corona
	Dam 2219 Three Parts Dark Buff Consort
Dam 2761 Heavily Variegated Buff Corona	Sire 1976 Heavily Variegated Buff Corona
	Dam 2190 Three Parts Dark Yellow Consort
Sire 4020 Variegated Buff Corona	Sire 3642 Heavily Variegated Buff Consort
	Dam 3413 Self Buff Corona
Dam 3914 Three Parts Dark Cinnamon Buff Consort	Sire 3786 Heavily Variegated Blue Corona
	Dam 3717 Heavily Variegated Buff Consort
Sire 3366 Heavily Variegated Buff Corona (c.c)	Sire 2786 Variegated Buff Corona (c.c)
	Dam 2671 Three Parts Dark Buff Consort
Dam 3223 Three Parts Dark Yellow Consort	Sire 2398 Heavily Variegated Buff Corona
	Dam 2647 Three Parts Dark Yellow Consort
Sire 4121 Three Parts Dark Blue Buff Consort (c.c.)	Sire 3786 Heavily Variegated Blue Corona
	Dam 3717 Heavily Variegated Buff Consort
Dam 3591 Heavily Variegated Buff Corona	Sire 3228 Lightly Variegated Buff Corona
	Dam 3190 Three Parts Dark Buff Consort
Sire 3712 Heavily Variegated Buff Corona	Sire 2836 Three Parts Dark Buff Corona
	Dam 3029 Heavily Variegated Buff Consort
Dam 3295 Self Buff Consort	Sire 2231 Three Parts Dark Yellow Consort
	Dam 2910 Heavily Variegated Buff Corona
Sire 2449 Heavily Variegated Buff Corona	Sire 2058 Heavily Variegated Buff Consort
	Dam 1733 Heavily Variegated Buff Corona
Dam 3866 Self Buff Consort	Sire 3099 Heavily Variegated Buff Corona
	Dam 3242 Self Yellow Consort

BREED: **GLOSTER CANARY**

RING NUMBER: **6176**

PARENTS	GRANDPARENTS	GREAT GRANDPARENTS
Sire 5104 Three Parts Dark Blue Buff Consort	Sire 4720 Heavily Variegated Buff Corona	Sire 4536 Heavily Variegated Buff Corona
		Dam 4369 Three Parts Dark Yellow Consort
	Dam 4077 Three Parts Dark Blue Buff Consort	Sire 3444 Three Parts Dark Blue Buff Corona
		Dam 3510 Heavily Variegated Buff Consort
Dam 5872 Heavily Variegated Buff Corona	Sire 5441 Heavily Variegated Buff Consort	Sire 5154 Three Parts Dark Buff Consort
		Dam 5147 Variegated Buff Corona
	Dam 5484 Variegated Buff Corona	Sire 5211 Lightly Variegated Buff Consort
		Dam 5277 Three Parts Dark Buff Corona

DESCRIPTION: THREE PARTS DARK BLUE CONSORT HEN

YEAR BRED: 1987

GREAT GREAT GRANDPARENTS	GREAT GREAT GREAT GRANDPARENTS
Sire 4172 Heavily Variegated Buff Corona	Sire 3141 Variegated Buff Corona
	Dam 3029 Heavily Variegated Buff Consort
Dam 3727 Three Parts Dark Buff Consort	Sire 1856 Three Parts Dark Buff Corona
	Dam 1808 Variegated Buff Consort
Sire 3980 Heavily Variegated Yellow Consort	Sire 2613 Heavily Variegated Buff Consort
	Dam 2787 Heavily Variegated Yellow Corona
Dam 3043 Heavily Variegated Buff Corona	Sire 2209 Heavily Variegated Buff Consort
	Dam 2646 Three Parts Dark Buff Corona
Sire 2978 Three Parts Dark Buff Consort	Sire 2025 Three Parts Dark Buff Corona
	Dam 2578 Three Parts Dark Yellow Consort
Dam 2912 Three Parts Dark Blue Buff Corona	Sire 2322 Three Parts Dark Blue Consort
	Dam 251 Three Parts Dark Buff Corona
Sire 3185 Heavily Variegated Buff Consort (c.c.)	Sire 2801 Three Parts Dark Blue Corona
	Dam 80 Three Parts Dark Cinnamon Consort
Dam 3309 Three Parts Dark Cinnamon Buff Corona	Sire 2274 Variegated Buff Corona
	Dam 2483 Three Parts Dark Yellow Consort
Sire 4399 Three Parts Dark Yellow Consort	Sire 3288 Heavily Variegated Buff Corona
	Dam 3164 Three Parts Dark Yellow Consort
Dam 4903 Three Parts Dark Buff Corona	Sire 3813 Three Parts Dark Buff Consort
	Dam 4605 Three Parts Dark Buff Corona
Sire 3180 Three Parts Dark Buff Consort	Sire 2613 Heavily Variegated Buff Consort
	Dam 2761 Heavily Variegated Buff Corona
Dam 4431 Variegated Buff Corona	Sire 4020 Variegated Buff Corona
	Dam 3914 Three Parts Dark Cinnamon Consort
Sire 4449 Heavily Variegated Buff Consort	Sire 3669 Heavily Variegated Buff Consort
	Dam 3801 Variegated Buff Corona
Dam 4532 Variegated Buff Corona	Sire 3884 Heavily Variegated Buff Corona
	Dam 3544 Lightly Variegated Buff Consort
Sire 4822 Three Parts Dark Yellow Consort	Sire 4337 Variegated Buff Corona
	Dam 4228 Three Parts Dark Yellow Consort
Dam 4693 Heavily Variegated Buff Corona	Sire 4604 Three Parts Dark Buff Corona
	Dam 80 Three Parts Dark Cinnamon Consort

183

BREED: GLOSTER CANARY

RING NUMBER: 6368

PARENTS	GRANDPARENTS	GREAT GRANDPARENTS
Sire 6098 Three Parts Dark Buff Consort (cinnamon carrier)	**Sire** 5456 Heavily Variegated Buff Corona	**Sire** 5154 Three Parts Dark Buff Consort **Dam** 5196 Variegated Buff Corona
	Dam 5678 Variegated Fawn Buff Consort	**Sire** 5059 Three Parts Dark Blue Buff Corona (cinnamon carrier) **Dam** 5221 Lightly Variegated Buff Consort
Dam 6047 Heavily Variegated Buff Corona	**Sire** 5549 Three Parts Dark Buff Consort	**Sire** 4533 Heavily Variegated Buff Consort **Dam** 4716 Three Parts Dark Buff Corona
	Dam 5361 Variegated Yellow Corona	**Sire** 4701 Three Parts Dark Yellow Consort **Dam** 4966 Variegated Buff Corona

DESCRIPTION: T. P. D. CINNAMON BUFF CONSORT HEN

YEAR BRED: 1988

GREAT GREAT GRANDPARENTS	GREAT GREAT GREAT GRANDPARENTS
Sire 4399 Three Parts Dark Yellow Consort	**Sire** 3288 Heavily Variegated Buff Corona
	Dam 3164 Heavily Variegated Yellow Consort
Dam 4903 Three Parts Dark Buff Corona	**Sire** 3813 Three Parts Dark Buff Consort
	Dam 4605 Three Parts Dark Buff Corona
Sire 3934 Variegated Buff Consort	**Sire** 3467 Variegated Buff Corona
	Dam 3544 Lightly Variegated Buff Consort
Dam 4692 Variegated Buff Corona	**Sire** 4227 Heavily Variegated Buff Consort
	Dam 4431 Variegated Buff Corona
Sire 4777 Three Parts Dark Blue Buff Corona (c.c.)	**Sire** 4411 Heavily Variegated Buff Corona
	Dam 4394 Three Parts Dark Fawn Consort
Dam 4425 Self Buff Consort	**Sire** 2808 Self Yellow Corona
	Dam 2797 Heavily Variegated Buff Consort
Sire 4965 Lightly Variegated Buff Corona	**Sire** 4449 Heavily Variegated Buff Consort
	Dam 4532 Variegated Buff Corona
Dam 4515 Three Parts Dark Buff Consort	**Sire** 3467 Variegated Buff Corona
	Dam 3190 Three Parts Dark Buff Consort
Sire 3884 Heavily Variegated Buff Corona	**Sire** 3099 Heavily Variegated Buff Corona
	Dam 2733 Three Parts Dark Buff Consort
Dam 3544 Lightly Variegated Buff Consort	**Sire** 1914 Lightly Variegated Buff Corona
	Dam 2810 Self Buff Consort
Sire 3274 Heavily Variegated Buff Corona	**Sire** 2238 Three Parts Dark Buff Corona
	Dam 2591 Three Parts Dark Yellow Consort
Dam 3727 Three Parts Dark Buff Consort	**Sire** 1856 Three Parts Dark Buff Corona
	Dam 1808 Variegated Buff Consort
Sire 4337 Variegated Buff Corona	**Sire** 3347 Heavily Variegated Buff Corona
	Dam 3772 Three Parts Dark Buff Consort
Dam 4228 Three Parts Dark Yellow Consort	**Sire** 3000 Three Parts Dark Buff Corona
	Dam 3164 Three Parts Dark Yellow Consort
Sire 4449 Heavily Variegated Buff Consort	**Sire** 3669 Heavily Variegated Buff Consort
	Dam 3801 Variegated Buff Corona
Dam 4532 Variegated Buff Corona	**Sire** 3884 Heavily Variegated Buff Corona
	Dam 3544 Lightly Variegated Buff Consort

Photographic Credits

Photos on the following pages are by C. B. Studios:
pp. 55, 56, 57, 102, 143. All others are by Dennis Avon.

Index

Numbers in *italic* refer to black and white illustrations.

Notes

Notes